Christopher Columbus

THE WORLD'S GREAT EXPLORERS

Christopher Columbus

By Zachary Kent

CHILDRENS PRESS ®
CHICAGO

Columbus embarking on his first voyage to the New World

Project Editor: Ann Heinrichs
Designer: Lindaanne Donohoe
Cover Art: Steven Gaston Dobson
Engraver: Liberty Photoengraving

**Library of Congress
Cataloging-in-Publication Data**

Kent, Zachary
   Christopher Columbus / by Zachary Kent.
      p.   cm. — (The World's great explorers)
   Includes bibliographical references and index.
   Summary: Examines the life of Columbus,
his journeys of exploration to the New World,
and his later years.
   ISBN 0-516-03064-7
   1. Columbus, Christopher—Juvenile
literature. 2. Explorers—America—Biogra-
phy—Juvenile literature. 3. Explorers—
Spain—Biography—Juvenile literature. 4.
America—Discovery and exploration—
Spanish—Juvenile literature. [1. Columbus,
Christopher. 2. Explorers. 3. America—
Discovery and exploration—Spanish.] I. Title.
II. Series.
E111.K35 1991   91-13863
970.01'5—dc20   CIP
[B]   AC

Oil painting of Columbus landing in the Americas

Table of Contents

Chapter 1
"Land! Land!"

The bright green water stretched in all directions. With endless rhythm, the rippling waves slowly rose and fell. Beneath the broad blue sky, three small ships rolled westward over the vast ocean: the *Niña*, the *Pinta*, and the *Santa María*. The square sails of the largest boat, the flagship *Santa María*, billowed in the breeze. The ship's captain stood upon the narrow wooden deck. For hours Christopher Columbus squinted his eyes, gazing at the empty horizon to the west.

Down in the hold, crewmen crouched together in the dark. They grumbled curses at their captain, calling him a fool, a madman, and a crazy dreamer. Above deck, high up in the rigging of the sails, other seamen sourly stared down at Columbus. Outside their captain's view, they made ugly gestures and muttered deadly threats.

These fearful Spanish sailors had not seen land for thirty days, and during that time thoughts of disaster filled their superstitious minds. One night they had seen a sudden flame streak through the sky. For many days the three ships had sailed through a strange, wide sea of floating weeds. The mysteries of the ocean frightened them. They were traveling into the unknown. The most uneducated sailors insisted the ships might reach the edge of the earth. Others worried that there would be no winds to blow the vessels back home. They would die of thirst and hunger, they swore, before they ever reached land again.

Finally the restless Spaniards could stand no more. On October 10, 1492, a group crossed the deck of the *Santa María* and roughly approached Columbus. Standing tall and firm, Columbus listened as they demanded that the ship turn around at once and return to Spain. If he refused, they threatened mutiny.

Instantly Columbus understood his grave danger. He looked at the scowling faces grouped around him and saw the anger in their eyes. Yet he remained calm and confident. Yes, they might kill him and turn the ships around, he warned. But if they returned to Spain, King Ferdinand and Queen Isabella would surely punish them with death. Speaking gently, Columbus next reminded the men of the great treasures that awaited them only a little farther to the west.

Still, the sailors grumbled unhappily. Finally Columbus threw back his shoulders. "There is no point in your complaining," he stated. "No point at all. I am going to the Indies and I shall sail on until, with God's help, I find them." He wanted just two or three more days to reach the Asian lands he was sure lay ahead. Then he would turn back if they wished.

Slowly the seamen returned to their duties. Some swore under their breath and shook their heads in dismay. Even the threat of death, it seemed, could not shake the iron will and confidence of Christopher Columbus.

The three small ships glided onward. Their sails fluttered and snapped with every gust. Salt water sprayed across their decks. Fretfully, the sailors reckoned they had sailed twice as far across the Atlantic Ocean as any European had ever gone before. Even the sight of birds sometimes winging overhead failed to give the men hope now. That night the crew solemnly whispered their prayers as if they expected disaster at any moment.

Sailors in unknown waters imagined that the sea held all kinds of frightful dangers.

Thursday, October 11, dawned with high winds and rough seas. The three ships plunged ahead on a west-southwesterly course, rocking hard and fast through every wave. In the sky more birds wheeled here and there. Sailors on the *Santa María* spied clumps of green seaweed beside their ship. Now, some men even smiled. Surely the sight of birds and seaweed meant that some land must be near. Perhaps they were not lost after all.

During the afternoon the seamen spotted further signs. Sailors on the *Pinta* noticed a reed and some sticks floating in the water. Crewmen on the *Niña* saw a thorn branch covered with red berries. The branch seemed to have been cut. "On seeing these signs, they all breathed again and were more cheerful," Columbus explained afterwards.

Columbus's ships: the Niña, *the* Pinta, *and the* Santa María

At sunset Columbus signaled his helmsmen to guide the ships on a course due west. Lookouts posted on the forward deck and high in the crow's nest of each ship gazed ahead with special keenness. King Ferdinand and Queen Isabella had promised a yearly gift of ten thousand Spanish coins to the first voyager who sighted land. With rising excitement, Columbus now promised to give a handsome silk doublet as well.

*Queen Isabella
of Spain with a royal page*

In the darkness the ships bounded ahead through the splashing waves. The fastest of the three, the *Pinta*, stayed always in the lead. On all the ships, few men slept that night. Ship's officers, able seamen, and cabin boys all stared westward, their hearts filled with thrilling expectations.

Pacing the deck of the *Santa María*, Columbus peered across the glinting waves. At 10:00 P.M. he suddenly called out. For a moment he thought he saw the faint flicker of a distant light, "like a little wax candle rising and falling."

During the next four hours, the three ships rolled farther ahead as the moon rose slowly in the sky. On the forward deck of the *Pinta*, lookout Rodrigo de Triana suddenly saw the distant outline of a white sand cliff gleaming in the moonlight.

"Land! Land!" the excited sailor shouted.

Martín Alonso Pinzón, captain of the *Pinta*, fired a small cannon as a signal for the other ships. On all three ships, wide-eyed sailors scrambled into the rigging and glimpsed the faint outline of land some six miles (ten kilometers) away. His emotions soaring, Columbus ordered that sails be lowered. The ships must wait for daylight before going farther. It would be a tragedy to crash upon some hidden reef with the lasting triumph of discovery now so very close at hand.

Carefully Columbus allowed the ships to drift toward the island's southern tip. In time, the light of dawn streaked across the water. Now the sailors more clearly saw the waves crashing on the distant shore. Beyond the shoreline rose the bright green of trees. For the first time in thirty-three days, these bearded sailors deeply breathed the sweet smell of land.

The ships raised sail and drew closer to the coast. Lookouts clung to the yardarms, shouting when they spotted underwater ridges of jagged coral. Leadsmen checked the depth of the water with weighted ropes. On the west side of the island, the little fleet at last dropped anchor within the safety of a cove.

On the three ships the common sailors chattered with excitement. Columbus and his officers dressed in their finest clothes of silk and velvet. Ships' boats splashed as deckhands lowered them into the water. Armed with swords, crossbows, and lances, the landing parties rowed toward shore. Each dip of the oars carried Columbus closer to the moment for which he had hoped so long.

Soon the boats dug into the sand. The eager sailors jumped into the water up to their knees. Holding aloft the royal standard of Spain, Columbus stepped onto the beach. Martín Alonso Pinzón, captain of the *Pinta*, and his brother Vincente Yáñez Pinzón, captain of the *Niña*, followed close behind. Each carried the banner of the expedition, a green cross on one side and crowns and initials symbolizing their king and queen, Ferdinand and Isabella, on the other.

With slow ceremony Columbus stepped across the wet sand. Tears of joy shone in his eyes. Dropping gently to his knees, he kissed the ground, claiming this land in the name of the Spanish monarchs. The

Banner of the expedition

island, one of a group today known as the Bahamas, he named San Salvador (Holy Savior) and asked the men around him to bear witness to the deed. Thereafter, the sailors respectfully addressed Columbus as Admiral of the Ocean Sea, for he had rightly earned that title. Those who had threatened mutiny now looked upon their leader with pride.

At the edge of the beach, native people stood naked and motionless among the palm trees. They watched for a time in silent amazement. Then with smiling innocence they clustered around the bearded strangers to see if they were real. "They were very well built," Columbus wrote, "with very handsome bodies and fine face. Their hair is coarse, almost like the hair of a horse's tail, and short."

"In order that we might win good friendship," Columbus later explained, "I gave to some of them red caps and to some glass beads, which they hung on their necks, and many other things of slight value, in which they took much pleasure." Pointing out to sea, the natives gestured that there were many other islands to the west and south. Columbus had promised to find the coast of Asia. Now he believed Japan, China, and India lay within his grasp. As the natives pressed close beside him, he named them Indians.

Through years of hardship, studying, planning, and waiting, Columbus never had lost hope. With unbreakable spirit the proud sailor refused to alter his vision of success. Even now, in his moment of great glory, he hardly dreamed he had failed to reach his goal. In a fabulous age of exploration Christopher Columbus would prove perhaps the greatest discoverer of all. By searching for a western route to Asia, he had chanced upon an entirely new world.

Columbus distributing hawks' bells and other gifts among the natives of Guanahani, which he renamed San Salvador

**Chapter 2
Son of Genoa**

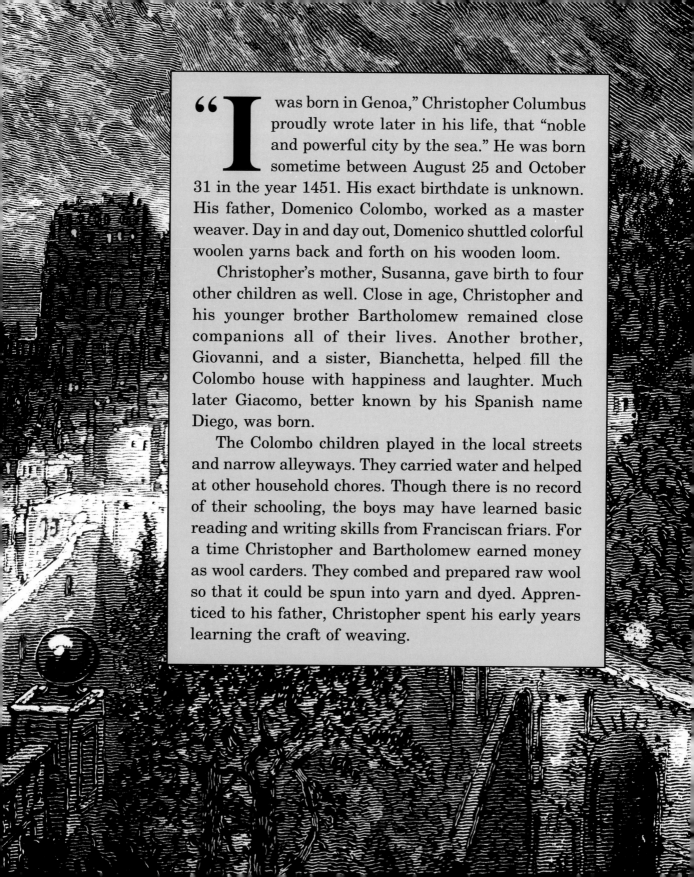

"**I** was born in Genoa," Christopher Columbus proudly wrote later in his life, that "noble and powerful city by the sea." He was born sometime between August 25 and October 31 in the year 1451. His exact birthdate is unknown. His father, Domenico Colombo, worked as a master weaver. Day in and day out, Domenico shuttled colorful woolen yarns back and forth on his wooden loom.

Christopher's mother, Susanna, gave birth to four other children as well. Close in age, Christopher and his younger brother Bartholomew remained close companions all of their lives. Another brother, Giovanni, and a sister, Bianchetta, helped fill the Colombo house with happiness and laughter. Much later Giacomo, better known by his Spanish name Diego, was born.

The Colombo children played in the local streets and narrow alleyways. They carried water and helped at other household chores. Though there is no record of their schooling, the boys may have learned basic reading and writing skills from Franciscan friars. For a time Christopher and Bartholomew earned money as wool carders. They combed and prepared raw wool so that it could be spun into yarn and dyed. Apprenticed to his father, Christopher spent his early years learning the craft of weaving.

The city of Genoa also taught the bright youngster many exciting and valuable things. The Colombos had named their oldest child after Saint Christopher, the ferryman, patron saint of travelers. Perhaps this very name helped shape the destiny of the weaver's son. There was no better place for a traveler to be born than in Genoa.

Located on the northwest coast of present-day Italy, Genoa thrived as a commercial seaport. Gulls swooped lazily over its great curving harbor. The briny smell of seawater drifted through the air. Dozens of ships rocked gently along the docks and wharves. Ships with sails unfurled came and went with every tide.

The harbor of Genoa buzzed with hints of the world beyond its horizon. Ship laborers unloaded heavy casks and chests filled with exotic trade goods. Shipwrights

The room where Columbus is said to have been born

hammered together graceful wooden hulls and fashioned tall ship masts. In taverns, bearded sailors loudly bragged of visits to foreign ports and fights with pirates. In small shops, mapmakers carefully sketched the coast and islands of the Mediterranean Sea.

Wandering along the docks and among the seaside streets, young Christopher Colombo could not help but learn about the sea. On the waterfront, people often recognized the weaver's son with his freckled face, blue eyes, and uncommon red hair. "At a very tender age," Columbus later wrote, "I entered upon the sea sailing." Perhaps a friendly fisherman let Christopher sail out and cast nets with him. Maybe a family errand carried the red-haired boy on a packet boat to the neighboring seaport of Savona. In time, people in Genoa wisely shook their heads. They guessed young Christopher would not follow the weaving trade. He loved the adventure of the sea too much.

In his earliest teenage years, Christopher took up the seafaring way of life. Possibly he traveled up and down the coast of Italy as a cabin boy aboard a merchant ship. On some voyages Bartholomew Colombo surely journeyed with his brother, for he loved the sailing life, too. Christopher's adventures carried him back and forth over the rippling waters of the Mediterranean Sea. Over the years, he traveled to Marseilles on the southern coast of France, Tunis in northern Africa, and the rocky Greek island of Chios. He learned how to tie sailors' knots, climb the rigging, and reef sails. His shipmates trained him to handle a tiller and read a compass. At night as he gazed into the starry sky, they taught him to name the constellations. In time, the young Genoese grew from a curious cabin boy into an able-bodied seaman.

Christopher as a youth

17

In May 1476, twenty-four-year-old Christopher Colombo again found work as a common sailor. He shipped aboard a Flemish merchant ship anchored in Genoa. Hauling high its sails, the vessel joined four armed Genoese ships bound for Portugal, England, and Flanders. The ships traveled together for greater safety. France, Genoa, and other Mediterranean lands were all at war just then. On August 13, the convoy passed along the southern coast of Portugal through the Strait of Gibraltar and into the Atlantic Ocean.

Disaster struck when a dozen French warships suddenly appeared on the horizon. In fierce attack, the French threw grappling hooks and ropes toward the Genoese ships in order to draw close to them and capture the convoy. All day the battle raged. The enemies slashed at one another with knives and swords. Arrows whizzed through the air. Thrown torches dropped upon the decks and set sails ablaze. By nightfall, four French ships had sunk and three of the Genoese ships were sinking, too.

On Columbus's ship, fire swept across the deck and burning masts crashed down. To save themselves, Columbus and his shipmates leaped into the water. While sailors drowned around him, Columbus grabbed an oar that floated past. By swimming and resting upon the oar, he slowly reached the coast of Portugal, some six miles (ten kilometers) away. At last, wounded and weary, he crawled ashore near the town of Lagos.

The citizens of Lagos nursed many of the survivors. In time, warm clothes, food, and kind treatment brought Columbus back to health. When he was well, he traveled to the nearby seaport city of Lisbon.

Without a penny in his pockets, Columbus needed work. At Lisbon he quickly signed aboard a ship bound for regions farther north. Perhaps the ship visited Bristol, England and Galway, Ireland. "I sailed in the year 1477, in the month of February, a hundred leagues beyond the island of *Tile*," Columbus later claimed. Tile, or Thule, was the name given to Iceland then.

Prince Henry the Navigator

After his icy winter visit into the North Atlantic, Columbus returned to Lisbon. Many Genoese bankers and merchants lived in Lisbon, and they welcomed Columbus into their midst. Already his brother Bartholomew worked there as a mapmaker. The red-haired sailor chose to make his home there, too, and joined his brother in the mapmaking trade. With plumed quill pens and colored inks, they drew the world's known islands and seacoasts from existing maps. Soon Columbus became such a skilled geographer that he could make his maps from memory.

Mapmakers often sold books as well. Possibly Columbus traveled across the plains and mountains of Portugal in order to sell leather-bound books in the cities of Spain. It is certain he learned Portuguese, Spanish, and even Latin, the international language of the Roman Catholic Church. His Italian name, Colombo, later became known as Colón in Spanish and as Columbus in Latin.

It was a curious twist of fate that had cast Columbus upon the shore so near to Lisbon after his sea battle. For a sailor, no more exciting city existed on earth. Prince Henry the Navigator, son of Portugal's King John I, had flourished between 1415 and 1460. Henry conducted a navigation school and encouraged his sea captains to explore west into the Atlantic Ocean and southward along the coast of Africa. Each new island discovered and every trading post established added to the power and riches of Portugal.

At least one summer voyage in 1478 carried Columbus to the Atlantic island of Madeira as an agent to buy a load of sugar. Romance, however, kept the twenty-seven-year-old in Lisbon during 1479. At the chapel he regularly attended, Columbus met twenty-four-year-old Felipa Moniz Perestrello, a member of a noble Portuguese family. Her father Bartholomew, now dead, had helped explore the Madeira Islands in 1425 and later had served as governor of the Madeira island of Porto Santo.

Courtship in the Middle Ages could be a very formal affair. Most likely, a chaperone watched over Christopher and Felipa whenever they sat or walked together. Felipa's widowed mother approved the match since Columbus was tall, handsome, and gentlemanly. He seemed so full of ambition. The Perestrello family was not wealthy, but Columbus expected no dowry from Felipa. In the summer of 1479, the two exchanged solemn wedding vows.

The newlyweds lived at first with Felipa's mother in Lisbon. The Widow Perestrello gave Columbus her husband's journals and sea charts, which he examined with great interest. In the next year the young couple sailed to the little island of Porto Santo, where Felipa's brother now served as governor. Cheerful toasts and joyful singing filled their home when their son Diego was born in 1480.

For three years Columbus made his home in the Madeira Islands, 400 miles (644 kilometers) off the West African coast. First he lived on Porto Santo and later at Funchal, the little capital of the Madeiras. As a mapmaker, sailor, and sometime merchant, Columbus earned his simple living. On one voyage he sailed to Guinea in West Africa. Along the famed "Gold

Columbus as a young man

Columbus in his study

Coast," he watched Portuguese ships collect rich cargoes of black slaves, spices, and gold. The new king of Portugal, John II, urged his sea captains to explore farther south along the African coast each year. He longed to discover an easy route to far-off India, where even more fabulous riches could be found.

In 1484, Columbus returned to Lisbon with his wife and young son. Sadly, however, while pregnant with another child, Felipa died. As Columbus watched his wife's burial in her family's chapel, surely he thought about his future. He could never be content as a part-time mapmaker and part-time sailor. A startling idea had been growing in his mind since his earliest days in Portugal. Given a chance, he was sure he could find the best ocean route to the Indies.

Chapter 3
The Enterprise of the Indies

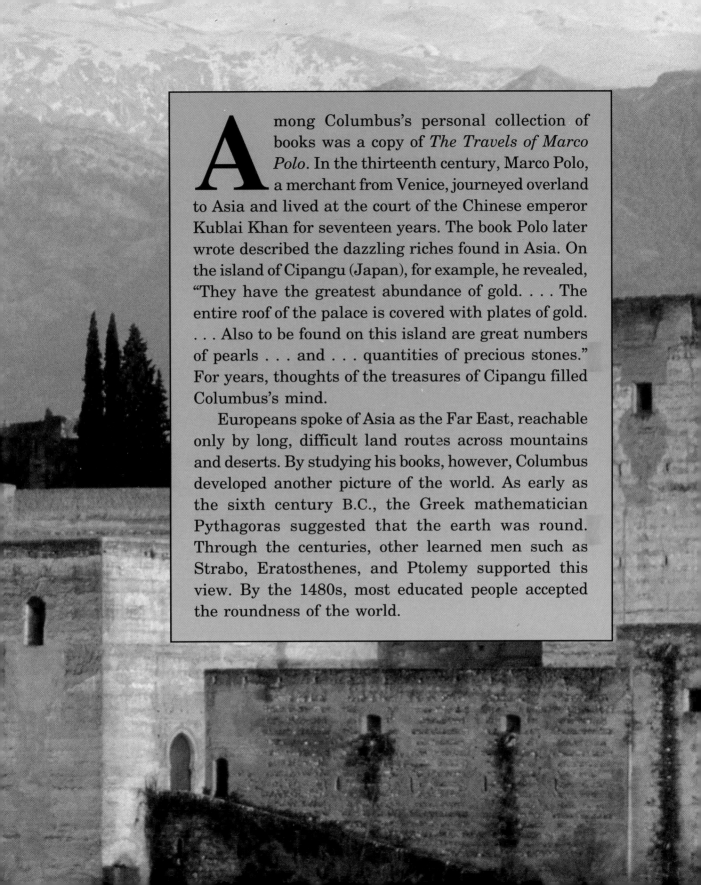

Among Columbus's personal collection of books was a copy of *The Travels of Marco Polo*. In the thirteenth century, Marco Polo, a merchant from Venice, journeyed overland to Asia and lived at the court of the Chinese emperor Kublai Khan for seventeen years. The book Polo later wrote described the dazzling riches found in Asia. On the island of Cipangu (Japan), for example, he revealed, "They have the greatest abundance of gold. . . . The entire roof of the palace is covered with plates of gold. . . . Also to be found on this island are great numbers of pearls . . . and . . . quantities of precious stones." For years, thoughts of the treasures of Cipangu filled Columbus's mind.

Europeans spoke of Asia as the Far East, reachable only by long, difficult land routes across mountains and deserts. By studying his books, however, Columbus developed another picture of the world. As early as the sixth century B.C., the Greek mathematician Pythagoras suggested that the earth was round. Through the centuries, other learned men such as Strabo, Eratosthenes, and Ptolemy supported this view. By the 1480s, most educated people accepted the roundness of the world.

Columbus himself had sailed south along the coast of Africa. He had traveled into the frozen waters to the north. The Atlantic Ocean was being explored in all directions, except to the west. Columbus joined those curious scholars and seamen who yearned to know what lay west beyond the ocean's broad horizon.

"Between the end of Spain and the beginning of India," predicted the ancient Greek thinker Aristotle in one of Columbus's books, "lies a narrow sea that can be sailed in a few days." For years Columbus gathered information to help prove this idea. In northern Europe, sailors told the saga of the Norseman, Erik the Red. In Viking ships Erik journeyed west from Iceland and discovered a place he called Greenland. A few years later, in about A.D. 1000, son Leif Eriksson sailed even farther westward. The Scandinavians claimed Eriksson landed on an island he named Vinland. Stories of distant continents and islands with such names as the Antipodes, St. Brendan's Island, Antilla, and Brazil had been passed along by sailors for centuries.

Real hints of land were added to the many rumors. While Columbus lived in Portugal, a captain named Vicente picked up a carved piece of wood floating far out at sea. Carved driftwood, thick pieces of bamboo, and strange floating beans sometimes drifted ashore on the Azores and Madeira islands. Two dead bodies with broad faces different than the Europeans' also washed ashore on the Azorean island of Flores. Poring over his collection of maps and books, Columbus dreamed of leading a westward voyage of discovery.

More and more, the idea filled him with eagerness and excitement. Columbus wrote to a Florentine physician named Paolo Toscanelli, who also believed

land could be found by sailing west. Toscanelli sent back a hand-drawn map and a letter. "I applaud your noble and grand desire to sail to the regions of the east by those of the west," the old doctor penned. "The voyage is not only possible to make, but sure and certain. . . . I am not amazed to see that you, a man of bold heart . . . are now aflame with zeal to undertake this voyage."

At last, armed with his maps and books and letters, Christopher Columbus sought an audience with King John II in 1484. Admitted before the Portuguese ruler, thirty-three-year-old Columbus proposed his project. He wished to sail west and reach the Indies by a direct route, if the king would only provide the ships. This Enterprise of the Indies, as Columbus called it, would surely yield the kingdom untold riches.

King John II listened carefully as the foreigner from Genoa earnestly talked on and on. Columbus boasted of his skills as a sailor and proudly demanded great rewards and honors for himself if he succeeded. Such boldness from a common sailor surprised the king. Portuguese historian João de Barros recalled that Columbus "was full of ideas and fancies about his island of Cipangu but had no proofs. The king accordingly did not put much trust in him."

A royal commission soon reported that Columbus's plan was impossible. The distance across the Atlantic was far too great. Already King John had spent chests of money sending ships to try to sail around the southern tip of Africa. He rejected the project.

Downheartedly Columbus walked the cobbled streets of Lisbon. But he refused to admit defeat. Out of work and deep in debt, he soon prepared his small son Diego for a sailing journey. Together they left Portugal early in 1485. Columbus had decided to try his luck in Spain.

Where the Tinto River joins the Saltes River on the Andalusian coast of Spain, father and son at last stepped ashore at the town of Palos. The high, whitewashed walls and red-tiled roofs of a Franciscan monastery called La Rábida stood on a bluff overlooking the Tinto River. Columbus knocked upon the gate and explained his mission in Spain. A kindly friar, Antonio de Marchena, arranged for Diego to attend school there while Columbus pursued his goal. "He alone never treated my ideas with ridicule," Columbus later remembered. The next few years would require every ounce of Columbus's patience. Not until May 1486 did the visionary sailor obtain his first interview with the king and queen of Spain.

Many separate kingdoms had sprawled across the countryside of the region we now call Spain before the 1400s. The marriage of Ferdinand of Aragon and Isabella of Castile in 1469, however, in time led to a united Spain. The young king and queen moved their royal court from city to city. By 1479, they had gained control over Spain's noblemen. Only the kingdom of Granada in the south remained in the hands of Moorish princes. The Moors, originally from North Africa, practiced the Islamic religion. By war or diplomacy, Ferdinand and Isabella vowed to place Granada under the banner of Spain and their own Christian faith.

Columbus with his son Diego at La Rábida laying plans for his voyage to the Indies

In the spring of 1486, the Spanish rulers brought their royal court to the city of Cordoba. War plans to win Granada filled much of Ferdinand's and Isabella's time. Among the people who petitioned them with requests, however, appeared the foreign sailor, Christopher Columbus.

Noblemen, waiting maids, and royal servants curiously eyed Columbus as he bowed low before the king and queen. When he rose to full height again, they noticed his fine figure, ruddy complexion, and fiery red hair. His clothes seemed plain, but his graceful manner showed he was a gentleman. Unrolling one of his maps, Columbus explained how the Indies could be reached by crossing the Atlantic. His blue eyes blazed with fervor as he asked for ships and royal support.

The daring idea aroused the monarchs' interest. The Genoese sailor certainly seemed sure of himself. But the king and queen knew little of geography. They ordered a commission of scholars headed by the friar Hernando de Talavera to study Columbus's proposal.

Portrait of Columbus with a beard

Month after month dragged by. At times Columbus stayed as a guest in the household of the friendly Count of Medina Celi. At other times he lived upon a small allowance granted by the king and queen. Hopefully he awaited an answer. In Cordoba he met a young peasant woman named Beatriz de Harana. Columbus's dream of becoming a respected, titled admiral prevented him from formally marrying this simple girl. The lonely widower, however, took Beatriz for his common-law wife. On August 15, 1488, the squealing cries of a baby announced the birth of Columbus's second son, Ferdinand.

Columbus explaining his plans to Ferdinand and Isabella

That fall Columbus impatiently returned to Portugal. Once more he hoped to interest King John II in his enterprise. He arrived in Lisbon just in time to witness the triumphant return of explorer Bartolomeu Dias. Dias had sailed around the southernmost tip of Africa, the Cape of Good Hope. His successful voyage gave the Portuguese an open ocean route to the Indies. Clearly King John no longer needed to consider Columbus's uncertain plan.

Although deeply disappointed, Columbus refused to give up. His brother Bartholomew still worked in Lisbon as a mapmaker. Columbus persuaded him to sail for England. Perhaps the English ruler, King Henry VII, would understand the benefits of sailing west and would lend a few ships for the project.

People of the Spanish royal court making fun of Columbus

The gray-haired Columbus

Columbus himself returned to Spain to await the decision of the Talavera Commission. These years proved the most difficult of his life. Nearly penniless, in threadbare clothes, Columbus followed Ferdinand and Isabella from city to city. Noblemen snickered whenever they saw the poor but proud adventurer hanging about the fringes of the royal court. They joked about his constant claims, which they believed wild and impossible. In time, the strain of waiting turned the color of Columbus's hair from red to gray.

Finally, in 1490, the learned scholars, geographers, and astronomers of the Talavera Commission announced their findings. A voyage across the Atlantic to the Indies could not succeed. Among their many objections, they claimed that the "uphill" return journey around the globe would be impossible. Most

Christopher Columbus with his sons, Diego and Ferdinand

importantly, they insisted the westward distance from Europe to Asia was far too great. Based on these arguments, Ferdinand and Isabella turned Columbus down. When they had won their war in Granada, perhaps they would consider his proposal again.

In frustration Columbus waited, staying with the Harana family in Cordoba and sometimes visiting his son Diego at La Rábida monastery in Palos. In the summer of 1491, Ferdinand and Isabella watched legions of Spanish infantrymen and troops of armored Spanish cavalrymen surround the walled city of Granada, the last stronghold of the Moors in Spain. During the long siege that followed, Queen Isabella kindly called Columbus back to her court outside Granada, sending him enough money to buy new clothes and a mule.

La Rábida monastery near Huelva, Spain, where Columbus planned his first voyage

31

On January 2, 1492, the Moors at last surrendered. Now all of Spain was reunited under the Catholic monarchs, Ferdinand and Isabella. During this time of victory, the king and queen again welcomed Columbus to their court.

For more than eight bitter years, Columbus had petitioned the royal courts of Portugal and Spain for help. Years of dashed hopes, scoffing remarks, and barely hidden smirks had deeply wounded his pride. By now Columbus believed he deserved great rewards. Ferdinand and Isabella listened in surprise as the poor Genoese sailor presented his proposal once again. He promised to reach the Indies, but he now demanded much larger payment for his services: at least one-tenth of all the riches he found in the Indies, the noble title Don, the rank of Admiral of the Ocean Sea, and the offices of governor and viceroy of the Indies.

The monarchs stared at Columbus in astonishment. "Even if the scheme were sound," Ferdinand Columbus later wrote of his father, "the reward he demanded seemed enormous." Ferdinand and Isabella refused to grant so much. Columbus withdrew from court with silent dignity. On the back of his mule, he soon trotted along the dusty road back to Cordoba.

Columbus had traveled no more than ten miles (sixteen kilometers) when a messenger galloped up beside him. Isabella desired that he return to court. At the very last moment, she had changed her mind.

Luís de Santángel held the position of Keeper of the Privy Purse, or royal treasurer. Santángel thought the king and queen foolish to refuse Columbus. This sailing enterprise would not cost so much money, and if Columbus succeeded, the gains would be very great indeed. The voyage could bring riches to the king and

The recall of Columbus

queen, help spread the Christian faith throughout the world, and bring everlasting glory to Spain. Santángel quickly persuaded Queen Isabella that Columbus should be given a chance to prove himself.

At Granada, Columbus learned that the monarchs now agreed to support his project. Santángel and several noblemen also supported it and invested some of the money needed. By April 17, 1492, the contract was signed with a flourish of signatures and wax seals. Columbus was granted all of his demands. The Genoese sailor was appointed admiral and viceroy "in all those islands and mainlands which by his labour and industry shall be discovered or acquired." He was given one-tenth in profits and other benefits as well. "By these presents we dispatch the noble man Christoferus Colón with three equipped caravels over the Ocean Seas toward the regions of India."

Chapter 4
The Niña, the Pinta, and
the Santa María

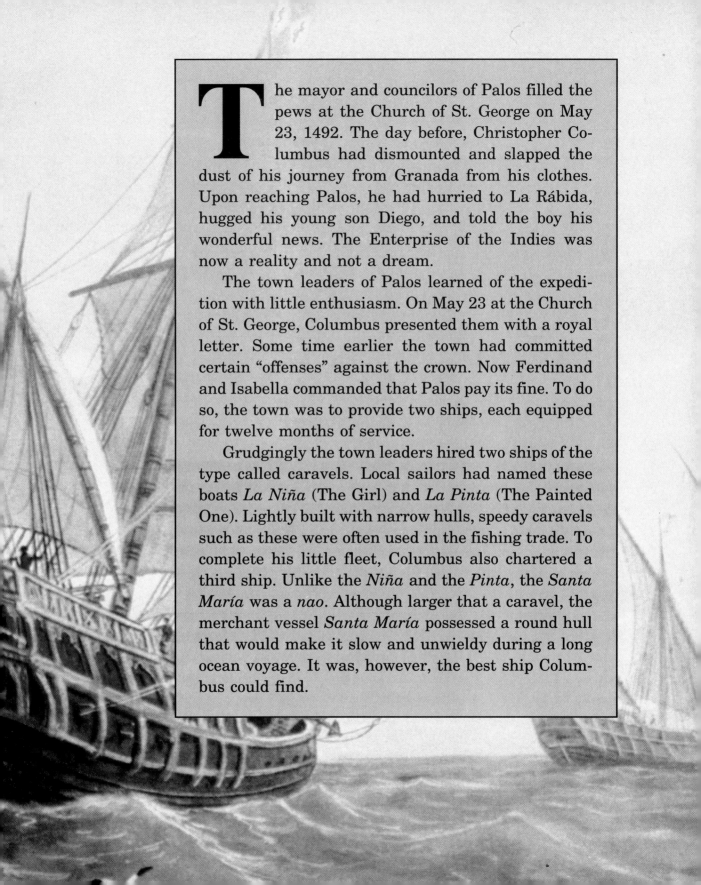

The mayor and councilors of Palos filled the pews at the Church of St. George on May 23, 1492. The day before, Christopher Columbus had dismounted and slapped the dust of his journey from Granada from his clothes. Upon reaching Palos, he had hurried to La Rábida, hugged his young son Diego, and told the boy his wonderful news. The Enterprise of the Indies was now a reality and not a dream.

The town leaders of Palos learned of the expedition with little enthusiasm. On May 23 at the Church of St. George, Columbus presented them with a royal letter. Some time earlier the town had committed certain "offenses" against the crown. Now Ferdinand and Isabella commanded that Palos pay its fine. To do so, the town was to provide two ships, each equipped for twelve months of service.

Grudgingly the town leaders hired two ships of the type called caravels. Local sailors had named these boats *La Niña* (The Girl) and *La Pinta* (The Painted One). Lightly built with narrow hulls, speedy caravels such as these were often used in the fishing trade. To complete his little fleet, Columbus also chartered a third ship. Unlike the *Niña* and the *Pinta*, the *Santa María* was a *nao*. Although larger that a caravel, the merchant vessel *Santa María* possessed a round hull that would make it slow and unwieldy during a long ocean voyage. It was, however, the best ship Columbus could find.

Both the *Niña* and the *Pinta* were vessels of about 60 tons (54 metric tons) each. (In nautical terms, this means that, when afloat, their hulls displaced about 60 tons of water.) From bow to stern on each, a sailor could pace no more than eighty feet (twenty-four meters). The *Santa María* might have been a 100-ton (90-metric-ton) ship, but its length was also about eighty feet. The draft of the ships, meaning the depth of their hulls under water, was probably about seven feet (two meters). The *Santa María* and the *Pinta* used square-rigged sails, while triangular or lateen sails hung from the *Niña*'s masts. These were the ships that rocked gently side by side in the harbor of Palos.

For ten busy weeks, laborers prepared the fleet for sea. Local chandlers sold Columbus necessary equipment, loading aboard ropes, sailcloth, block and tackles, anchors, planking, and tools. Armorers hefted onto deck small swivel cannons called lombards and falconets, and bakery workers rolled great barrels of biscuits up the gangways. Wine, olive oil, salted pork, rice, and cheese were purchased and stored away, enough for a long voyage. For trading purposes, Columbus filled chests with colored glass beads and shiny brass rings. Perhaps the natives of the Indies would also like the jingle of little hawks' bells and the bright red color of knitted wool sailors' caps. He loaded chests of these items, too.

With his great purse of Spanish maravedis and golden escudos provided by the king and queen, Columbus easily purchased his supplies. Hiring his ships' crews proved more difficult, however. In the taverns of Palos and nearby towns, sailors drank wine and scornfully discussed the expedition. Sailing westward into unknown seas seemed total madness! Worse yet,

Statue of Martín Alonso Pinzón in Palos de la Frontera, Spain

the voyage would be commanded by a foreigner who had never even been captain of a ship before! It was true many sailors were out of work, but the risk of sailing on these ships seemed too great.

Luckily for Columbus, at least one Palos citizen gladly joined the enterprise. During his travels as a merchant sea captain, Martín Alonso Pinzón had seen maps of the world. The same stories of the Indies that thrilled Columbus aroused Pinzón as well. In the central square of Palos, Pinzón addressed his fellow townsfolk. "Come away with us, friends," he urged. "You are living here in misery. But come away with us on this voyage and, according to certain knowledge, we shall find houses roofed with gold and all of you will return prosperous and happy."

Because they trusted Pinzón, about ninety crewmen and cabin boys signed on. Columbus chose to sail aboard the largest ship, the *Santa María*. He picked Pinzón to captain the *Pinta* and Pinzón's younger brother, Vicente Yáñez Pinzón, to command the *Niña*.

At long last the moment for departure arrived. Before dawn on August 3, 1492, forty-year-old Christopher Columbus knelt in the Church of St. George and prayed for the success of the enterprise. A boat soon carried him to the *Santa María*. Upon deck, Columbus ordered anchors weighed and sails unfurled. The three small ships started down the Tinto River. With the turn of the tide at sunrise, the wind blew them into the widening ocean.

The fleet's first goal was to sail southwest to the Canaries, islands settled by Spaniards off the West African coast. During these first days, Columbus carefully observed how the ships handled at sea. The round-bellied *Santa María* was the slowest of his ships. In the shifting winds of the open seas, he also noticed that the lateen sails of the *Niña* were sometimes hard to control. On the fourth day out, heavy seas violently rocked the ships. Suddenly the rudder of the *Pinta* jolted out of its sockets. Straining sailors tied ropes to hold the rudder in place until repairs could be made.

Finally, on August 11, the ships reached the Canaries. The fleet spent nearly a month among these islands. On the *Pinta,* crewmen hammered and properly fixed the rudder into place. On the *Niña,* sailors rehung the rigging so that square sails could be used. Rowing ashore, the seamen refilled barrels with fresh water, collected firewood, and purchased fresh meat from Spanish settlers. One night near the island of Tenerife, the crewmen shuddered with ter-

Vincente Yáñez Pinzón,
captain of the Niña

ror. They stared as flames suddenly erupted from a mountaintop. Columbus had seen volcanoes before while sailing in the Mediterranean. He explained the sight to his crews and tried to calm their fears. Some superstitious sailors, however, muttered that the shooting flames were a bad sign indeed.

Volcanic landscape of Tenerife, one of the Canary Islands

Columbus scoffed at such talk. He had important reasons for traveling by way of the Canary Islands. The ships would not be welcome at the Portuguese islands of the Madeiras and the Azores. Those islands were too far north for Columbus's purposes anyway. In that region, the trade winds most often blew to the northeast. Ships could not sail west into the wind. During his voyage down the African coast in the 1480s, however, Columbus had noticed that farther south, a change in winds and currents would allow boats to sail westward. Using this valuable information, he picked the Canaries as his starting point.

On September 8, a cooling breeze flapped the sails of the *Niña*, the *Pinta*, and the *Santa María* to life again. Columbus ordered a course due west, and the ships made steady progress. The next day, the Canaries disappeared behind them. From that moment onward, the ships sailed through unknown waters.

In his cabin Columbus kept a daily journal of distances and directions traveled. In 1492 the art of navigation remained very simple. Columbus most likely relied on his mariner's compass and his skills at "dead reckoning." A magnetized needle kept the northern point of the compass card always seeking the earth's northern magnetic pole. By reading his compass and carefully guessing the speed of the ships and the ocean currents, Columbus plotted his positions on his charts.

From the very start, Columbus decided to keep two separate logbooks. In the book he showed his sailors, he wrote daily distances that were less than his actual reckoning. He used this trick "so that the crews should not lose heart or be alarmed if the voyage grew too long." Ironically, Columbus often overestimated the reckoning of his ships' speed. As a result, the false log he showed his sailors was more correct than his secret log.

During the first days of the voyage, the ships ran smoothly westward. The crews performed their duties with skill and in good faith. Boatswains shouted orders and barefoot sailors climbed into the rigging to trim sails. On deck, men scrubbed the planking clean, spliced rope, sewed torn canvas, and tended fishing lines. Cooks kept small fires burning in sandboxes and brewed pots of porridge, soup, and stew. After

Map showing the route of Columbus's first voyage

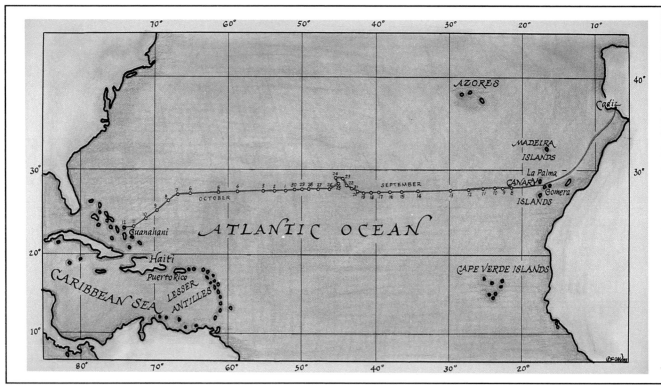

sunset, the night watch paced the decks. Cabin boys closely watched the sand pour through half-hour glasses and at the last second turned them over to start anew. On deck, pilots watched their compasses, while below deck helmsmen held the tillers. Together they kept the course that never changed—west.

In ten days, the three ships sailed a distance of over 1,100 nautical miles (2,039 kilometers). In warm sunshine and shimmering moonlight the ships rolled onward. The wind always pushed from the stern. Small birds soared high overhead. Flying fish and black-backed dolphins arched out of the water. The brightness of the sea and sky and the fresh smell of the air filled Columbus with joy. "It is like April in Andalusia. Nothing is missing except the nightingales," he cheerfully wrote in his journal. "How great a pleasure is the taste of the mornings."

Columbus on shipboard

A ship in the Sargasso Sea

Not everyone aboard the ships shared the captain-general's feelings. On the night of September 15, a sudden flame streaked across the sky and dropped into the distant sea. Few of the crewmen knew about meteors. They worried that the strange sight might be a sailors' warning.

The next day the bows of the ships cut through tufts of floating seaweed. The green carpet of weed stretched in all directions as far as the eye could see. They had entered that region of the Atlantic called today the Sargasso Sea. Sargasso weeds are harmless algae. The Spanish sailors, however, had never seen such a thing before. For several days the ships easily plowed a path across the great weed mat, while anxious sailors murmured that perhaps the ships had traveled too far.

Pinzón mistakes clouds for land.

West of the Sargasso Sea the direction of the wind began to vary. The ships' lookouts saw a whale, dolphins, flying fish, a pelican, and other smaller birds, but still no sight of land. Now the seamen grew more restless. Columbus sometimes heard their grumbled complaints behind his back.

Often Martín Alonso Pinzón sailed the speedy *Pinta* in advance of the other ships. He wished to win the great prize of ten thousand maravedis that Ferdinand and Isabella had offered to whoever sighted land first. As the sun set on September 25, Pinzón suddenly cried out from the *Pinta*'s poop deck, "Land, land, sir! I claim the reward!" For hours Columbus excitedly sailed the fleet toward the distant shape. The land, however, proved to be nothing but a low formation of clouds.

This disappointment caused the crewmen to mumble curses and complain more loudly. Already this voyage had lasted longer than any they had ever undertaken. Fearful men wept that they would never see land again. It was dangerous to sail so far west, they said. Perhaps a crack in the earth would suck the ships under the sea. Perhaps a watery monster would rise up and devour them. These superstitious sailors let their minds run wild.

On October 7 the *Niña* fired a signal gun. Sailors aboard hoisted flags, believing they had sighted land. The farther they sailed, however, the more their spirits fell. What they thought was land faded and disappeared. This second false moment of hope left the crews feeling more gloomy than ever. Later in the day, land birds were seen flying toward the south-

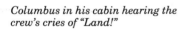
Columbus in his cabin hearing the crew's cries of "Land!"

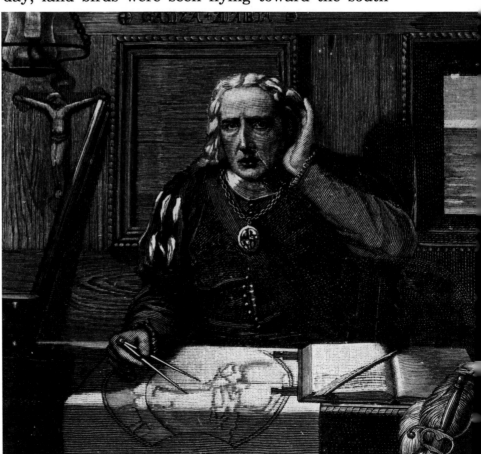

west. "Those birds know their business," remarked Martín Alonso Pinzón to his men. Columbus agreed to alter the fleet's course and follow in that direction.

During the next two days, flocks of ducks flew overhead. Colorful songbirds sometimes hovered around the ships before winging away. With a strong breeze, the boats made good speed. At any moment Columbus sensed that land would appear.

The simple Spanish sailors on the three ships refused to share their leader's hopes. There was no land. For thirty days they had seen none. In small groups they whispered threats and plotted mutiny. They desperately yearned to turn back toward home. On October 10 Columbus revealed in his journal, "Here the men could now endure it no longer. They complained of the long voyage."

Columbus observing birds as he watches for land

Columbus facing his mutinous crewmen

Standing on the deck of the *Santa María*, Columbus stared into the eyes of the seamen crowded around him. Although they could kill him in an instant if they chose, he never flinched. He had worked too hard and long to turn back now. He could not be swayed even by the threat of death. Instead he joked with the men. He reasoned with them. He made stubborn threats of his own. They must go on just a little farther, for the glory of their church and for their king and queen. Unhappily the sailors returned to their posts. None dared to challenge Columbus further. With muttered curses they placed their fates in his hands.

Through the next day, October 11, fragrant breezes puffed the ships' sails and hurried the fleet ahead

Joy on shipboard at the first sighting of land

over bounding waves. Birds flew here and there in greater numbers. Seaweed and even a few twigs floated near the ships. These signs surely revealed that land was near. Columbus ordered the ships to steer due west again. Crewmen hauled on sheets and braces. All eyes excitedly gazed to the west.

At 10:00 P.M. Columbus believed he saw a distant light. Other crewmen were not so sure. Lookouts rubbed their eyes and continued staring. Below deck, helmsmen held the course and eagerly listened for news. On every ship hopes rose higher and higher, until at last, at 2:00 A.M. on October 12, Rodrigo de Triana, a lookout on the *Pinta*, loudly cried, "Land! Land!"

Chapter 5
"Come and See the Men Who Have Come from Heaven"

On the morning of October 12, 1492, natives on the island of Guanahani stepped from their thatched huts. Some stared with dreamy wonder, while others froze in total fear. To them it appeared that three floating islands filled the nearby cove, and white clouds hung fixed among the branches of the islands' trees. The natives crept forward and watched as boats started toward the shore. Strange, bearded men wrapped in colorful cloth stepped onto the beach. Falling to their knees, these long-haired, white-skinned men chanted in a curious language and gestured solemnly with their hands.

Having renamed the island San Salvador and offered prayers of thanks, Christopher Columbus rose to his feet. With broad smiles, his Spanish crewmen now addressed him as Don Christopher, admiral, governor, and viceroy. His heart pounded with pride, for true to his word, he had found land by sailing west. Gladly he turned and met the natives who shyly walked toward him. He gave them glass beads and red woolen caps to show his friendly intentions. "Afterwards," Columbus wrote, "they came swimming to the ships' boats, where we were, and brought us parrots and cotton thread in balls, and spears and many other things."

These natives were members of the Taino culture of the Arawak language group. But Columbus called them Indians, for he truly believed he had reached the Indies. During his first day at San Salvador, he observed them with curious delight. "They all go naked as their mothers bore them," he noted in his journal. "Some of them paint their faces, some their whole bodies, some only the eyes, and some only the nose. They do not bear arms or know of them; for I showed them swords, and they took them by the blade and cut themselves through ignorance."

Word of the fantastic visitors spread quickly across the entire island. On the morning of October 13, hundreds more natives hurried to see for themselves. "They came to the ship in boats, which are made of treetrunks like long boats, all of one piece," described Columbus. "They propel them with a paddle, like a baker's shovel, and they travel wonderfully fast." Columbus and his fellow Europeans were seeing their first canoes.

On the morning of October 14, Columbus and some crewmen curiously rowed north along the shore in the ships' boats. Where they passed native villages, the people always came running. "Some of them . . . threw themselves into the water and swam up to us," revealed Columbus, "and we understood that they asked us if we had come from heaven. One old man got into the boat, and several shouted to the rest both men and women, 'Come and see the men who have come from heaven; bring them food and drink.'" This, at least, is what Columbus imagined they said.

Whenever he traded with the natives, Columbus tried to find out if they had gold. "I saw that some of them wore a small piece hanging from holes in their noses," he wrote, "and from signs I was able to under-

Model of a Taino Indian

Columbus and his crew on the island he named San Salvador

stand that in the south there was a king who . . . possessed much of it." Columbus forced several natives onto his ships to act as guides, and on the afternoon of October 14 his crews hoisted canvas once more. During the next twelve days, the Spanish fleet sailed southwest among other islands in that group known today as the Bahamas.

Santa María de la Concepción, Fernandina, and Isabela were the names Columbus gave the next three islands he landed upon. The Arawak natives fled among the trees whenever the strange ships appeared. Friendly gestures and the calls of the captive Indians aboard sometimes brought canoes paddling cautiously near. Gifts of beads and other trinkets never failed to dazzle the native people.

Angel fish

The Spaniards were often equally amazed. Gazing into the clear blue water, Columbus exclaimed, "There are fish here so different from ours that it is a marvel . . . blue, yellow, red, and all the colors of the rainbow." On Fernandina the sailors came upon some unusual pets—dogs that never barked. In the huts they also discovered woven cotton nets hanging from post to post. The natives slept in them and called them *hamacas.* In the ships' cramped quarters, sailors would soon find hammocks useful and comfortable.

Nature on the islands also greatly impressed the explorers. Strange flowering trees and shrubs filled the air with sweetness. "These islands are so lovely," declared Columbus, "that I do not know where to go first." Songbirds chirped in every tree and brightly feathered parrots flew in such thick flocks they seemed to darken the sun. Columbus and his men were surprised by the strange sight of a large, snakelike creature. "When it saw us," Columbus exclaimed, "it threw itself into the lagoon and we went after it, for the water was not very deep, until we killed it with our spears." The sailors removed the horrible animal's skin to take back to Spain. Before long, though, they would see many more of these creatures, for they were iguanas, very common on those islands.

Unhappily, Columbus discovered very little gold. His sailors only obtained by trade the few golden nose ornaments the natives sometimes wore. Still he remained brimming with hope. Eager to please, the natives spoke of a larger island farther to the southwest called Coiba, or Cuba. They promised Columbus he would find plenty of gold there. Sure that they described Cipangu, the admiral steered in that direction and on October 28 reached the coast of Cuba.

Green iguana

An island off the Cuban coast

Sailing along the shore, they saw only a few native huts among the palm trees. No traces of the riches of Cipangu could be seen. At last they anchored near a river Columbus named the Río de Mares (River of the Seas). Now he began to think they had reached the coast of mainland Asia instead of Cipangu. The coast seemed far too long to belong to an island. Conversations with frightened and amazed natives yielded confusing information. When they pointed toward the island's interior saying "Cubanacan," Columbus imagined they were referring to the Chinese emperor Kublai Khan. Though that ruler had lived two hundred years earlier in Marco Polo's time, perhaps this was his successor, another Great Khan.

The Chinese emperor Kublai Khan

Columbus sent two of his men, Luis de Torres and Rodrigo de Jerez, hiking into the mountains to find the court of the Great Khan. Meanwhile, the rest of the crew beached the three ships in order to make repairs. Sailors careened the hulls, scraping away weeds and barnacles. They caulked leaks between the planks and tarred over wormholes. Strong thread and sharp needles patched weak canvas. Sailors' callused hands spliced frayed ropes whole again.

In their free time the men explored the immediate neighborhood. Local natives offered the adventurers a tasty root they called *mames*, the common sweet potato. Finally, on November 5, Torres and Jerez returned from their inland journey. They had found nothing but jungle villages and no sign of the Great Khan. Curiously, however, they described a native habit they observed. These Cuban Indians often carried rolled tubes of dried leaves. With the tubes lit on fire, they sucked the smoke into their nostrils or mouths. The tubes were called *tobacos*. In future years Europeans would call the leaf tobacco, and the smoking habit would spread throughout the world.

Having failed to find cities of gold on Cuba, Columbus ordered his ships to sea again. He understood from his captive Indians that two islands, Bohio and Babeque, lay to the east. By gestures the natives indicated that the people of Babeque gathered gold nuggets on their beaches.

Wishful thoughts of gold and glory now filled Captain Martín Alonso Pinzón's head. On November 21, he suddenly decided to sail the *Pinta* off on its own. The slow *Santa María* could not keep pace, and Columbus angrily watched as the deserting ship gradually disappeared beyond the horizon. "He had done

Columbus meeting with the natives of Hispaniola

and said many other things to me," Columbus bitterly complained in his journal. With just the *Niña* and the *Santa María*, he sailed on through the uncharted waters.

In time, the two ships drew near the coast of Bohio (present-day Haiti). Great forests of fir trees stood in the foothills along the coast. The trees, the birds, the fish, and flowers all reminded Columbus of Spain. Therefore he named the island La Isla Española (The Spanish Island), later known as Hispaniola.

Columbus's Indian guides nervously warned that the natives on this island were cannibals who roasted and ate the flesh of their enemies. When the ships touched land, however, the natives fled in terror or greeted the explorers with friendliness. Gifts of colored beads and hawks' bells soon brought out thousands of people. They paddled up in canoes to trade for trinkets or simply swam out for a closer look at the men who came from the sky. "I cannot believe that any man has ever seen people with such good hearts," declared Columbus. Local chieftains sent gifts of peace, including belts decorated with beaten gold, and Columbus hoped that at last he had reached Cipangu.

Day after day the *Niña* and the *Santa María* sailed eastward along the island's northern coast. Carefully the ships weaved among the rocks and reefs beneath the surface. On December 24, they neared the coastal village of a chieftain named Guacanagari. During the previous forty-eight hours, Columbus had guided the ships up the uncharted coast without a wink of sleep. As the hour reached midnight, the start of Christmas Day, the weary admiral retired to his cabin.

The *Santa María* rocked gently forward, following in the wake of the *Niña*. A light breeze, smooth water, and the glimmering moon all had a very soothing effect. First Juan de la Cosa, officer of the deck, abandoned his post and went to bed. Soon afterwards, with lazy yawns, the helmsman handed the tiller to one of the cabin boys and also nodded off to sleep.

At midnight a gentle bump suddenly awakened Columbus. He heard the cabin boy shouting. Rushing onto deck, the admiral discovered the *Santa María* had run onto a reef. The wooden hull scraped harder upon the underwater coral with every rhythmic swell.

Wreck of the Santa María *on the coast of Hispaniola*

Immediately Columbus ordered Juan de la Cosa and other sailors into the ship's boat. He told them to drop an anchored rope far astern, so that the *Santa María* could be hauled off the reef. Instead the panicked sailors rowed away toward the safety of the *Niña*.

Already the tide was on the ebb, falling shallower with each wave. Columbus ordered the main mast cut down to lighten the endangered ship. Still it would not move, except to tilt slowly to one side. The *Niña* arrived, but too late to help. The *Santa María* sagged heavily onto the coral and began to crack up. "Her seams opened," Columbus sadly declared, "and the water began to come in. . . . I saw no chance of saving my ship, and to spare the lives of my crew I left her and went with them to the *Niña*."

On Christmas morning, 1492, Columbus stood upon the crowded deck of the *Niña*, hardly believing his misfortune. The wreck of the *Santa María* reduced the size of the fleet to just one ship. The friendly chieftain Guacanagari sent his people at once to help with their canoes. Together Spaniards and natives unloaded as much as they could from the *Santa María* and carried the cargo ashore. "Not so much as one shoe-lace was missing," remarked Columbus in praise of the honest natives. To cheer up Columbus, Guacanagari presented him with gold masks, necklaces, and rings. By gestures, the native people described mines of gold that could be found in an inland mountain region called Cibao.

Throughout Christmas Day Columbus reflected on his situation. He now wished to sail back to Spain to report on his discoveries. But with only one ship, he would have to leave some men behind on Hispaniola. Soon he convinced himself that God had given him a sign. "The Lord," he explained, "had ordained this shipwreck so that he might choose this place for a settlement. . . . Without this I would not have been able to leave people here, nor to provide them with so much equipment, weapons and supplies." Overnight the fateful wreck of the *Santa María* changed Columbus from an explorer into a colonizer.

The admiral named his colony La Navidad (Christmas) in honor of the holiday. "I have now given orders for a tower and a fortress to be built," he noted in his journal. "And they have timber to build the entire fortress, and supplies of bread and wine for more than a year, and seed for sowing. . . ." Altogether some thirty-five men volunteered to stay.

Through the next days the sound of axes rang through the trees. Excited by thoughts of the golden

Indians bringing provisions to Columbus's shipwrecked crew

riches of Cibao, the Spanish settlers quickly erected their little fort. Others loaded wood, water, and food aboard the *Niña*. Before leaving, Columbus gave the natives a demonstration of Spanish power. He fired the guns on the *Niña*, sending the cannonballs smashing through the wrecked hull of the *Santa María*. Sternly he promised that he would one day return to see that the settlers remained safe and sound. On January 4, 1493, the *Niña* at last set sail. On deck Christopher Columbus waved farewell to the brave men of La Navidad.

Chapter 6
Homeward Bound

One lonely ship sailed east along the coast of Hispaniola. Strong headwinds blew into the faces of the crew, and the *Niña* made slow progress. On January 6, however, a lookout gladly shouted. The *Pinta* was sailing west along the coast to meet them.

Soon Martín Alonso Pinzón climbed aboard the *Niña*, where Columbus greeted him with smoldering anger. Pinzón apologized and offered excuses for having deserted the fleet. The winds, he claimed, had drawn the *Pinta* off to Babeque (Great Inagua Island), where he stayed to search for gold. Finding very little, he had sailed on to Hispaniola next. Columbus suspected Pinzón of jealousy and greed. For the sake of peace, however, he agreed to overlook the captain's disloyalty.

The seamen caulked leaks and made other ship repairs during the next two days. While filling water barrels in a nearby river, sailors thought they saw flecks of gold. Columbus named the river the Río de Oro (River of Gold). Rowing near the river's mouth the admiral claimed he saw three mermaids rise out of the sea. "They are not as beautiful," he wrote in his journal, as pictures of mermaids he had seen. Most likely these "mermaids" were sea mammals called manatees, whose faces sometimes do look human.

Many people believe that sailors mistook manatees (above) for mermaids, although it is hard to see why.

Mountaineer of Hispaniola's interior regions

Hoisting sail, the *Niña* and the *Pinta* journeyed eastward. On January 13 they approached shore again to collect fresh drinking water. Here they met unfriendly natives for the first time. With smoke-stained faces and feathered hair, these natives waved clubs and fiercely ran forward with bows and arrows. The seven Spaniards who had landed on the beach defended themselves. They slashed one native with a sword and struck another with a crossbow arrow. The fifty attackers quickly scattered into the woods. Columbus guessed that these Indians were Caribs, the cannibals he had heard about. In future years, this entire sea would come to be called the Caribbean.

On January 16 the two ships at last sailed beyond the sight of land. Columbus would have been happy to stay and look for more islands. But his leaking ships and restless crews persuaded him it was time to start the homeward voyage.

During the first days at sea, the trade winds forced the ships in a northerly direction. After two weeks, they reached the latitude where the currents changed. Now the ships plowed eastward, their sails full of air like great puffed cheeks. At high speeds the *Niña* and the *Pinta* raced through this uncharted region.

The helmsmen steered a steady course, and the farther they traveled the more wintry the weather turned. Then on February 12 the sea grew rough and cold rains made the crewmen shiver. Soon howling winds ripped first in one direction and then another. To escape the full fury of the awful storm, the seamen lowered all canvas but the mainsails. Fierce waves pitched into both ships and lightning cracked the sky. The helmsmen could barely control their tillers. They had to run with the tempest wherever it took them.

Through the next day the green, foaming sea still splashed across the decks. The ships bucked and bobbed through each curling wave. That night, flares were lit so that the ships might stay together in the dark. The light from the *Pinta*, however, grew fainter and fainter. By the morning of February 14, the *Pinta* had disappeared.

Alone again, the *Niña* rolled roughly through the stormy sea. Soaked to the bone, sailors worked the pumps below deck. With every wave it seemed the little ship would tip. Putting his faith in God, Columbus suggested the crew conduct a lottery. He marked a pea with an *X* and threw it and other peas into a sailor's cap. Whoever picked the marked pea would make a pilgrimage to a blessed Spanish shrine if they safely reached home. Drawing first, Columbus fatefully picked the crossed pea.

A great tidal wave threatens to overturn the ship.

Still the storm tossed the *Niña* without mercy. The fearful crew conducted two more lotteries. Seaman Pedro de Villa chose the crossed pea in one drawing. Admiral Columbus picked it again in another. On behalf of the crew, they vowed to visit churches and offer special Masses if the *Niña* were spared.

When the awful storm continued, the men fell to their knees and prayed. Crying aloud, they all swore they would humbly attend church as soon as they safely reached land. Finally by the end of the day the sea grew less violent. Sighs of relief turned to shouts of joy on the morning of February 15. A speck of land stood on the horizon straight ahead. The storm had swept the *Niña* to the island of Santa Maria in the Azores.

On February 19, the admiral sent half of his thankful crew ashore. Barefoot and dressed only in their long shirts, these sailors made solemn steps toward a chapel on the island to fulfill their religious vows.

The Portuguese governor of Santa Maria, however, promptly arrested the ten men. He hardly believed the stories the sailors told about the Indies. He guessed these Spaniards had been trading illegally in Portuguese territory on the coast of Africa. Shouting from the deck of the *Niña*, Columbus refused to surrender himself and the rest of his crew. He and the Portuguese governor argued and exchanged threats for several days. At last the captive Spaniards were released. The *Niña* was permitted to continue on its way toward Spain.

For three days the little ship made smooth progress. Then on February 27, the wind grew wild and the ocean turned rough again. Shrieking gusts ripped the

Columbus's ships threatened by stormy seas

Niña's sails to ribbons. Icy water flooded below deck. "When we were at the very doors of home," declared Columbus, "it was more than sad to encounter such a storm."

Again the crew drew lots to chose someone to make another religious pilgrimage if they were spared. For the third time, Columbus himself picked the marked pea. But for days the weather stayed fierce in spite of prayers and vows.

Spanish historian Bartholomew de las Casas later copied Columbus's journal. The March 4 entry read in part:

"Last night they went through so terrible a storm that they thought they were lost, for the seas went over the ship from both sides and the winds seemed to lift her into the air . . . and so things went on until the first watch, when the Lord showed him land and the sailors saw it. . . . When dawn came he recognized the coast, with the Cintra mountains, near the Lisbon river." This miserable winter storm had tossed the *Niña* to Portugal instead of Spain. Glad for any sight of land, Columbus sailed the *Niña* into Rastelo harbor near Lisbon.

First to board the little Spanish ship was the famous Portuguese explorer Bartolomeu Dias. Excitedly Columbus described his great discoveries to the west. He showed his travel documents from the Spanish king and queen. He paraded his captive Indians upon the deck.

Soon the skeptical people of Lisbon were convinced. They crowded to the riverfront to gaze at the *Niña*. Curiously they swarmed aboard to see and touch the Indians and hear the sailors' wonderful stories of the Indies.

Learning of Columbus's astounding travels, King John II called him to his court. By mule Columbus traveled beyond Lisbon to the monastery where the Portuguese king was staying.

"The king received him," wrote historian Las Casas, "with all due honour and was very courteous, bidding him be seated."

How satisfying a moment this must have been for Columbus, who twice had had his enterprise turned down by King John II.

Happily Columbus recounted his spectacular voyage and showed some of the gold he had collected. He had brought a few of his Indians to the court, and using beans they easily created a map of their islands on a table.

Rastelo harbor in Lisbon

Quickly King John II realized the extent of the new discoveries and the promise of wealth they held. The Portuguese king could hardly hide his feelings at losing such wonderful lands.

"O, man of little understanding!" King John cried out. "Why did you let such an enterprise fall from your hands?"

With good grace, the king allowed Columbus to depart. At Rastelo the damaged *Niña* had been repaired. On March 13, a light breeze carried the caravel out to sea again. The coast of Spain lay close at hand. On the afternoon of March 15, 1493, the sailors of the *Niña* proudly unfurled flags and pennants. A lombard cannon cracked a loud salute to announce the ship's return to the Tinto River. After 224 days of travel, the *Niña* returned to its home port of Palos. By a seeming miracle, the *Pinta* arrived a few hours later.

Chapter 7
Triumph and Tragedy

The people of Palos wildly cheered and tears streamed from their eyes. Husbands, sons, and fathers had returned from the unknown. The storm had swept the *Pinta* all the way to the northwestern coast of Spain. Upon reaching land, Martín Alonso Pinzón had sent a letter to King Ferdinand and Queen Isabella announcing the great discoveries. He offered to come immediately to court and make a full report. By messenger the monarchs politely replied that they would wait to hear from Columbus himself.

The hardships of the voyage had ruined Pinzón's health. Now he had been snubbed by the king and queen. Sailing home to Palos, the sea captain could not hide his envy of Columbus. Weak and bitter, Pinzón returned to his country estate, where he died within three weeks.

The other sailors of the *Niña* and the *Pinta* meanwhile enjoyed the welcome of heroes. In Palos and neighboring towns, citizens threw banquets and parties in their honor. Everyone listened in wonder at their stories of strange lands and fantastic sea adventures. Ferdinand and Isabella promptly sent Columbus a letter full of praise and invited him to their court at the city of Barcelona.

With some of his crew and all of his Indians, the triumphant admiral began his 800-mile (1,287-kilometer) journey to Barcelona. In the cities of Seville and Cordoba, the proud procession stopped for celebrations. All along the route, people leaned from windows, crowded doorways, and lined the road. Some glimpsed the shining gold ornaments Columbus displayed. Others grinned at the brightly feathered parrots in cages or gaped at the six copper-skinned Indians. Wonders such as these had never before been seen in all of Europe. Word of the newly discovered route to the Indies quickly traveled from country to country. The name Christopher Columbus was fast becoming famous.

At last in April the great explorer paraded into Barcelona. To honor his arrival, the city was decorated with festive banners and streamers. Noblemen met the admiral on the road and respectfully escorted him to court. When Columbus entered the royal courtroom, Ferdinand and Isabella rose from their thrones. He knelt to kiss their hands, and they asked that he rise and sit beside them as a special honor.

In the hushed courtroom, Columbus told the story of his voyage from start to end. He brought forward his Indians for all to see. His men carried in the parrot cages and opened chests containing cotton, spices, strange lizard skins, and native bows and arrows. Columbus described in detail the lush resources of the islands. Finally he presented the king and queen with the gold he had collected: decorated masks and belts, gold nuggets, and gold dust. Ferdinand and Isabella dropped to their knees and wept with joy. With deep faith they thanked God for bestowing such good fortune upon Spain.

A portrait of Columbus that was commissioned by Queen Isabella

Columbus enters Barcelona after his first voyage.

The king and queen granted Columbus all the titles they had promised: admiral, viceroy, governor. They also gave their new knight Don Christopher a family coat-of-arms to prove his noble rank forever. During the next days Columbus savored life as a guest at court. Whenever the king went horseback riding he invited Columbus to ride beside him, a very high privilege indeed. When he walked in public, people thronged around him. With contented smiles, the gray-haired admiral repeated his stories of golden cities. Those who listened excitedly dreamed of seeing the Indies for themselves.

Already, plans for a second voyage were rapidly going forward. Columbus had proved the Indies could be reached. Now Ferdinand and Isabella realized they must quickly take full possession of this newfound region. King John II had decided to claim all of the lands touching the Atlantic for Portugal. He sent his appeal to the Pope in Rome, the highest authority among Catholics in the world. Unhappily for the Portuguese king, the decision of Pope Alexander VI gave Spain the right to all areas explored in the western Atlantic. As a compromise, Spanish and Portuguese diplomats eventually signed the Treaty of Tordesillas in 1494. It set the dividing line between the two nations' empires along a point 370 leagues (about 1,100 miles [1,770 kilometers]) west of the Cape Verde Islands.

Pope Alexander VI, who arranged the division of the New World between Portugal and Spain

Long before the signing of that treaty, however, Columbus had departed from Spain. From May to September 1493, he organized the gathering of ships and equipment at the great Spanish seaport of Cádiz. The huge fleet of seventeen ships filled the wide harbor. Among them bobbed the trusty *Niña*. Laborers loaded barrels of wine and salted meat into cargo holds. Crewmen hoisted aboard sailing gear, weapons, trade goods, building tools, and sacks of grains and seeds for planting. For the settlement of Hispaniola, colonists herded onto the decks cattle, donkeys, goats, and squawking chickens.

Map showing the division of the world according to the Treaty of Tordesillas of 1494

Columbus had no trouble finding men willing to join this grand expedition. Sailors, craftsmen, farmers, surgeons, and soldiers all eagerly signed aboard. A cavalry troop of twenty lancers brought their horses onto deck. Several missionaries headed by Friar Bernard Buil would go to convert the "heathen" Indians to the Christian faith.

Hundreds of "gentlemen volunteers" also wished to join the voyage. Columbus agreed to let over two hundred come along. Among these adventurers was Columbus's young brother Diego. Another was Juan Ponce de León, the future discoverer of Florida. Altogether, some 1,500 sailors, colonists, and government officials embarked upon the seventeen ships.

On September 25, 1493, Cádiz church bells rang. After praying for the success of the expedition, citizens hurried to the harbor. Sailors and colonists hugged friends and loved ones good-bye. Cannon thundered and trumpets sounded in final salute. Bright breezes filled the painted sails of the great fleet. The flag of Spain fluttered from the stern of every ship. At last the assorted vessels stood out to sea.

Juan Ponce de León

The departure of Columbus on his second expedition

Admiral Columbus chose a 200-ton (179-metric-ton) caravel for his flagship on this second voyage. Its name was the *Santa María*, but it was commonly known as the *Mariagalante* (The Gallant Maria). From the deck of the *Mariagalante*, Columbus proudly watched the progress of his fleet. Calm weather carried the ships first to the Canary Islands. After gathering fresh supplies, the fleet then steered southwest into the open ocean.

Warming sunshine, blue skies, and puffy clouds lay overhead, while the ships plunged forward through the salty waves of the green ocean. Neither the great matted weed of the Sargasso Sea nor a sudden electrical storm on October 26 much altered the fleet's speed or course. The admiral's Indians, five of whom were

Map drawn in the 1700s, showing the Caribbean islands Columbus explored

sailing with the fleet, had described a string of islands southeast of Hispaniola. Now curiosity drew Columbus toward that unexplored island region, known today as the Lesser Antilles.

Few sailors doubted Columbus now. They trusted in his proven navigating skills to find land. Seaweed and flying flocks of birds provided the admiral with his clues. On the evening of November 2, he ordered all ships to slow by shortening sail. In the gray light of early morning on Sunday, November 3, a lookout on the *Mariagalante* suddenly cried out, "Land! We have land!" The word spread to every ship. Sailors and passengers excitedly pushed to the rails. Just twenty-two days after leaving the Canary Islands, here was land again.

Columbus named this mountainous island Dominica, after the Latin word for Sunday. Unable to find a suitable harbor at Dominica, the fleet sailed northward. Another small island soon appeared, which Columbus named Mariagalante after his flagship. Accompanied by a number of officers and gentlemen, Columbus stepped ashore. In formal ceremony they knelt together, and Columbus claimed the land for Spain. It seemed no natives lived on Mariagalante. Curiously the Spaniards scrambled along the beach and among the trees and bushes. A few men soon learned that unexpected dangers lurked in this strange new world. Biting into a fruit that looked like an apple, their tongues and mouths instantly burned with awful pain. They had tasted the zanilla apple, or machineel. The Carib natives used the fruit's milky sap to poison the tips of their arrows.

The next morning the fleet sailed north to the next island in the curving chain. Columbus gave this island the name Santa María de Guadalupe. The Carib natives of Guadalupe were nowhere to be seen. Possibly they were away on a raiding expedition. The curious Spaniards walked through their villages and poked into their abandoned huts. With interest they examined hammocks, cotton cloth, pottery, and tamed parrots. Some brave men tasted a prickly-skinned fruit they found and smiled happily at its sweetness. It was the pineapple. Most of the Spaniards shuddered with disgust, however, as they looked around. Everywhere they found human bones and skulls, ugly evidence that the Caribs were indeed cannibals.

At last the fleet sailed onward. Between November 10 and November 14 the ships passed several small islands, and Columbus named them all. Now steering

Blue and gold macaw

westward, the ships eventually dropped anchor at an island the admiral called Santa Cruz, or Holy Cross, known as St. Croix today.

"On one of the days while we lay at anchor," remembered adventurer Michele de Cuneo, "we saw coming round a point a *canoa.* . . ." Upon seeing the amazing fleet, the Caribs in the canoe tried to paddle away. Cuneo and other Spaniards quickly rowed a ship's boat in pursuit. "As we drew near," explained Cuneo, "the Caribs began to shoot at us with their bows, and half of us would have been hit if it had not been for our shields. But I have to tell you that an arrow came at a sailor with a shield and it pierced the shield and went three inches into his breast, so that within three days he was dead." The Spaniards killed one of the Caribs and captured the others during this bloody encounter.

Pressing northward, the wind carried the fleet to a group of lovely little islands. Columbus named this enchanting group the Eleven Thousand Virgins after an early Christian legend about St. Ursula and her young women followers. Today they are still called the Virgin Islands. To the west Columbus next named the island of Gratiosa to honor the mother of a friend. Beyond that, the fleet touched upon the coast of a much larger island. The admiral named it San Juan Bautista (St. John the Baptist). In 1508, Juan Ponce de León would return to conquer this island. It would become better known as Puerto Rico.

Eager to reach the colony he had founded at La Navidad, Columbus refused to tarry long. On the horizon to the west lay the coast of Hispaniola. The seventeen ships scudded westward over the water along the island's northern coast, and Columbus soon recognized familiar reefs and coves. On November 25 the fleet neared the Río de Oro, where Columbus had seen the flecks of gold. He sent a boat rowing up the river's mouth. Excitedly this shore party expected to find La Navidad colonists busily collecting gold along the riverbank.

Instead they discovered the rotting bodies of four men. A rope was knotted around the neck of one man. The feet of another were tied together. The thrill of reaching Hispaniola suddenly changed to worry. Columbus directed his captains to sail on to La Navidad. They reached the bay on the evening of November 27. Instead of glad shouts, signal fires, and canoes full of friendly natives, only darkness and silence greeted them.

The next morning the voyagers discovered that their worst fears were true. The fortress of La Navidad lay in a ruin of charred wood and ashes. Hardly a trace of the Spanish settlers could be found. The first European settlement in America had been wiped out.

Timidly a few natives from Guacanagari's village stepped forward from the jungle and told the story of what had happened. After the *Niña* left, the settlers had quarreled among themselves and split into rival groups. One gang hiked into the mountains, roughly demanding gold and native women wherever they went. A fierce chieftain named Caonabo finally struck back. Caonabo and his warriors killed the gang of Spaniards and then marched to the coast, where they burned the Navidad settlement and slaughtered every settler.

Aboard the anchored ships, the stunned Spaniards muttered among themselves. Columbus had promised them a paradise where gentle Indians would treat

Columbus finds the bodies of some of his slain men at La Navidad.

them like gods. Instead, their countrymen had been murdered on this hostile island. In order to put the tragic memory of La Navidad behind them, Columbus sailed the fleet east along the coast in search of a new place for settlement. Fighting headwinds all the way, it took the ships a month to travel barely forty miles (sixty-four kilometers). Men fell ill, livestock died, and food spoiled. Unable to wait any longer, Columbus landed at the first satisfactory harbor. In a sheltered cove the fleet dropped anchor on January 2, 1494. Here Columbus established his new colony, and he called it Isabela, in honor of the Spanish queen.

Chapter 8
The Noble-Hearted Admiral

The tropical sun burned the colonists' fair skin and rainstorms left them soaked and chilled. Clouds of mosquitoes bred in nearby marshes and stagnant pools swooped upon the Spanish laborers. Squirming and scratching at itchy bites, many men fell sick with malaria. Still, the work to build the town of Isabela progressed. The colonists planned streets and started erecting a church, a military storehouse, and simple dwellings. Farmers hoed gardens and planted seed.

The sad memory of La Navidad lingered, of course, and Columbus clearly recognized the need for positive action. On February 2, he ordered twelve of the fleet's idle ships to sail home to Spain. Under Captain Antonio de Torres, Columbus sent loads of sandalwood timber, cargoes of cinnamon, peppers, and other spices, sacks of spun cotton, and samples of glittering gold. Still, Columbus feared the voyage was not showing a profit, so he also sent twenty-six Indians as slaves.

Next, Columbus made war against the fierce chieftain Caonabo. Leading five hundred of his healthiest men, Columbus marched from Isabela on March 12. He intended to conquer the mountain region of Cibao and at last discover the mines. For days the soldiers of fortune stepped over rocky jungle trails and waded rivers. "We experienced . . . terrible weather, bad food, and even worse drink," wrote Michele de Cuneo, "yet the hunger for gold gave us strength and speed."

With trumpets blaring and bright banners waving, the army entered the mountains. The astonished Indians offered no resistance. Instead they stared in wonder or quaked with fear. Men on horseback especially alarmed them. They believed the snorting horse and the armored lancer upon its back were together one horrifying animal.

In the mountains of Cibao, Columbus established a wooden fort he called St. Thomas. The fort would protect the Spaniards he would assign to develop the mines. In the meantime, Columbus left fifty-six men under the command of Pedro Margarit to trade for gold with local natives.

Columbus building the fort of St. Thomas in the mountains of Cibao

Columbus arrived back at Isabela with his weary army on March 29. Unfortunately, the town had not flourished while he was away. Dozens of feverish settlers had died. Worse still, the entire colony seemed on the verge of starvation. Even in the rich, black soil of Hispaniola, untended vegetables wilted. None of the colonists was very interested in farming. They wished instead to snatch the gold of Hispaniola and quickly return to Spain. Many openly resented the hardships of settlement. Crimes against Indians rose as greedy colonists tried to fulfill dreams of wealth. As governor and viceroy, Columbus ordered some Spaniards whipped and others hung. Discontented colonists soon hated their Genoese lord, and the strain of governing these wild adventurers left Columbus exhausted.

The town and colony of Isabela, founded by Columbus

A second large army expedition seemed to solve some of the admiral's troubles. Over three hundred boisterous Spaniards commanded by Alonso de Hojeda eagerly marched off to explore the island and conquer hostile natives. As for himself, Columbus prepared three of his remaining ships, the *San Juan*, the *Cordera*, and his favorite, the *Niña*, for sailing. The duty of governing Hispaniola he would leave to his young brother Diego. Clearly Hispaniola possessed no civilized cities of gold. Now Columbus was determined to sail west and explore Cuba more carefully. Having promised to find the riches of Asia, he hoped that course would lead the way.

On April 24, 1494, the fleet sailed west from Isabela, and four days later the green coast of Cuba lay in sight. The three ships bounded along the southern Cuban coast, and on April 30 they anchored overnight in a great beautiful bay. The admiral named it Puerto Grande (present-day Guantanamo Bay).

*Sandy beach, sparkling water, and
deep-blue sky of the Caribbean*

During the first lovely days of May, the fleet glided farther westward through sparkling blue and green waters. The breeze carried with it the delicious scent of trees and flowers from the land. Another great bay soon opened along the shoreline and Columbus named it Santiago. From a thousand huts, natives rushed to the beach to gaze at the approaching ships. The Spaniards rowed boats ashore and traded trinkets for bits of gold. These natives spoke of an island to the south called Jamaica where gold was plentiful. Leaving Santiago behind, Columbus steered south to find this island of gold.

Strong winds and rough seas drove them to Jamaica. The beauty of its high mountains and lush forests greatly impressed the sailors. The warlike behavior of the natives soon led to violence, however. These Indians wore feathered headdresses and palm-leaf skirts. They paddled handsomely carved canoes. When the Spaniards attempted to land, the warriors hurled spears and threw stones. Fighting back, Spanish crossbowmen sent arrows flying and killed perhaps a dozen people. Then the Spaniards let loose a big, ferocious dog that chased the stunned survivors.

The next day, the defeated natives returned and begged for mercy. Columbus showed them some gold, but they had no idea what it was. After stopping at a bay known today as Montego Bay, Columbus chose to return to Cuba and further explore its coast.

A rough storm blew the three ships back toward Cuba. Amidst the bad weather, Columbus neared the coast on May 14 at a point he called Cabo de Cruz (Cape of the Cross). The next days called upon his great skills as a navigator. The admiral's son Ferdinand later explained, "The greatest problem was

Montego Bay, Jamaica

that the entire sea to the north and northwest was full of innumerable small islands. Some were wooded, but most of them could hardly be seen above water." Columbus named the region the Queen's Garden. For eight days the ships carefully threaded their way among these dangerous islands.

When they finally sighted the coast of mainland Cuba again, the ships edged westward, always keeping land in view. This uncharted region proved every bit as hazardous as the Queen's Garden. Shallow waters and narrow channels demanded total alertness. For weeks Columbus seldom rested. Instead he shared every hardship of his crews. Michele de Cuneo reported: "There has never been a man so noble-hearted and so proficient in the art of navigation as the said Lord Admiral. For while navigating, he could say, just by looking at a cloud or a star at night, what was going to happen, or if bad weather was to come. He kept his share of the watch, and took his turn at the helm, and when a storm had passed, he set the sail while the others slept."

Hungry and weary, by June 12 even Columbus had had enough of Cuba. The men had seen such wonders as bright pink flamingos for the first time. But the golden cities of China had not appeared.

Still stubbornly insisting that Cuba was part of mainland Asia, though he was still on Cuba's southern coast, Columbus turned the ships back in the direction of Hispaniola. On June 30 the *Niña* scraped to a halt in shallow water. Working hard with cables and anchors, the sailors luckily pulled the ship free. Weeks of difficult sailing against headwinds and through another awful storm finally brought the battered little fleet back to the point called Cabo de Cruz.

Caribbean flamingos

Indians bringing gifts of food to the Spaniards

Friendly natives fed the Spaniards fruit, fish, and bread made from the cassava root while they rested for four days. Then, making best use of the winds, the fleet crossed south over the waves to Jamaica again. Rounding the island's westernmost point, Columbus spent the first weeks of August mapping Jamaica's southern coast before heading for Hispaniola.

Michele de Cuneo was the first crew member finally to sight Hispaniola on August 20. Columbus named the point Cabo de San Michele Saonese in honor of a friend. From here the admiral sent nine men hiking overland toward Isabela to report that the ships were safe. At the same time, he sailed eastward exploring Hispaniola's southern coast. The work of charting these waters ruined Columbus's health. Near Mona Island, between Hispaniola and Puerto Rico, he suddenly fell gravely ill. In his cabin bed, he blindly

Bartholomew Columbus

tossed and turned with a burning fever. His crews decided to make haste and return to Isabela. Five days later, on September 29, they sailed into port.

For many months Columbus lay in a deathlike coma. Only slowly did he regain his senses. One of the first faces he recognized was that of his brother Bartholomew, whom he had not seen since sending him to England many years before. In the wake of the great seventeen-ship fleet, other caravels were sailing to Hispaniola bringing colonists and supplies. Highly favored as the admiral's brother, Bartholomew had received command of three caravels. Loaded with food and supplies, the three ships sailed to Isabela at the end of spring 1494. Columbus granted his brother the high title of *adelantado*. Through the next months, as the admiral was nursed back to health, Bartholomew governed Hispaniola as his second-in-command.

While Columbus had been away exploring Cuba and Jamaica, riot and turmoil had ruled Hispaniola. Pedro Margarit had taken control of the roving Spanish expedition. Hunger and greed drove this army from one Indian village to another. Instead of treating the peaceful natives with kindness and consideration, the Spaniards soon fell to plundering their huts and kidnapping their women.

Rather than submit, growing numbers of Indians revolted. Harshly treated natives ambushed wandering bands of Spaniards on mountain trails. Vengeful Spaniards in turn committed new outrages, and the island sank into a state of bloody chaos.

Already Columbus had sent his brother Diego back to Spain with 1,500 Indian slaves. At that time, it was a lawful, accepted practice to enslave people captured in battle. In March 1495, Columbus organized a new military expedition to restore order on Hispaniola. His health restored, the admiral led two hundred crossbowmen and musketeers out of Isabela. Twenty lancers trotted on horseback and twenty dogs panted along the trail. Many Indian allies commanded by Guacanagari also joined the march.

Massed in the great valley below Cibao, thousands of native warriors were preparing an attack on Isabela. Fearlessly Columbus attacked the Indians instead. The Spanish force charged out of the woods from all directions, trumpets blaring. Hearing noise from all sides, the Indians panicked and fled. Crossbow arrows whistled and muskets cracked and flamed. Horsemen galloped among the Indians, wildly thrusting their lances, and barking bloodhounds snapped at legs and heels. Hundreds of Indians were killed in this battle and many more were captured.

To punish the defeated natives of central Hispaniola, Columbus soon devised a tax. Every Indian over fourteen years old was required to pay enough gold every three months to fill a hawk's bell. This system of taxes enslaved the conquered Indians. In Cibao, they labored daily beside the riverbanks panning and digging for gold. Many overworked Indians died of exhaustion, disease, and starvation. Some hid in the mountains only to be hunted down by the Spaniards and their sniffing dogs. Others committed suicide to escape their misery. Between 1494 and 1496, one-third of Hispaniola's native population—some 100,000 of 300,000 people—died.

Indians forced to pan for gold

Having established a cruel peace on Hispaniola, the Spaniards were struck by a natural disaster in June 1495. A terrible storm the Indians called a *huracan* (hurricane) swept across the island. The blasting wind and rain tore up trees and destroyed houses in Isabela.

The storm also sank three of the four ships in the harbor. Only the *Niña* survived. Using pieces of the wrecks and cutting down timber, colonial shipwrights built another caravel. Columbus named it *Santa Cruz*, but the sailors nicknamed it the *India*. This was the first European-style ship ever to be built and launched in the Indies.

Relief ships from Spain arrived in October. They brought bad news from court for Columbus. Pedro Margarit, Friar Buil, and other returned colonists had reported to the king and queen. They had complained about Columbus, his colonial government, and living conditions on Hispaniola. Columbus realized he must hurry to Spain and defend his reputation.

By March 1496, the *Niña* and the *India* were ready to sail. Crewmen carried aboard chests of gold and cotton Columbus had collected. Spanish passengers and Indian slaves also were crowded aboard the little ships.

During the long voyage to Spain, the *Niña* and the *India* stopped at the island of Guadalupe again to collect food and water. A fierce crowd of Carib women fired a shower of arrows at the Spaniards and tried to prevent their landing.

Among Europeans, there existed an ancient legend about the land of Amazon, where women ruled and lived like men. Columbus concluded that these Carib women were the Amazons.

Caribbean Indians in a battle with Spaniards

At last, on April 20, the two ships sailed into the open sea. Columbus avoided the storms of the North Atlantic by sailing along a more southerly route. Contrary winds, however, kept the ships at sea so long that food supplies ran low. Nearly starved, crews and passengers gladly cheered at the sight of land.

After fifty-three days, the *Niña* and the *India* dropped anchor at Cádiz on June 11, 1496. Columbus and his crew had been away from Spain for two years and nine months.

Chapter 9
Voyage to Another World

"I saw him at Seville on his return, dressed almost like a Franciscan friar," recalled historian Bartholomew de las Casas. If Columbus had failed King Ferdinand and Queen Isabella in some way, he wished to show his deep regret. Wearing simple religious clothes, he walked the streets of Seville until summoned to the royal court being held in the city of Burgos.

Proudly Columbus journeyed to Burgos, leading a cavalcade of Indians and Hispaniola treasure. At court he happily embraced his two growing sons, who were serving there as royal pages. Ferdinand Columbus long remembered his father's formal entrance into the courtroom of the king and queen:

"On arrival at Burgos he was well received by the Catholic Sovereigns, to whom he presented a great quantity of things . . . from the Indies, including various birds, animals, trees, and plants . . . many masks and belts with plates of gold . . . and gold dust in its natural state, fine or large as beans and chickpeas and some the size of pigeon's eggs."

Columbus, dressed in a friar's garb, arriving at Burgos after his second voyage

Columbus glowingly described the discoveries of his second voyage and told the king and queen of his progress in taming Hispaniola. He also reported that Isabela was being abandoned in favor of a better harbor on the southern coast of the island. He had ordered the construction of a new capital town to be called Santo Domingo.

Columbus again promised Ferdinand and Isabella the riches of Asia, and they still trusted him in spite of the many complaints they had heard. Therefore, they agreed to his proposal for a third voyage of discovery. It took some time to launch this third expedition. European diplomacy and the expensive royal marriages of their children with foreign dukes, princes, and princesses kept the Spanish rulers fully occupied. The *Niña* and the *India* sailed for Hispaniola in

January 1498 carrying valuable supplies for the colony. Columbus, however, stayed behind. Having requested six more caravels, he spent months at the monastery of Las Cuevas in Seville waiting for a reply.

At last the king and queen provided Columbus with enough money to assemble his fleet. Fewer men wished to sail with the famed admiral now. Stories of the hardships on Hispaniola and the lack of easy riches had spread across Spain. To help raise crews Ferdinand and Isabella granted pardons to jailed debtors, thieves, and other criminals willing to sign aboard.

Aboard three of his ships, Columbus organized craftsmen, miners, soldiers, and farmers, and also thirty women. These supply vessels would sail directly to Hispaniola. The remaining three ships Columbus reserved for exploration. Two of them were caravels named *El Correo* and *La Vaquenos*. The flagship was a round-bellied *nao* named the *Santa María de Guia*.

At the end of May 1498, land breezes puffed the sails of the readied fleet. The six ships glided from the harbor of Seville and down the Guadalquivir River to the Spanish coast. From the Canary Islands the three supply ships steered westward, while from the Portuguese Cape Verde Islands Columbus guided the exploration ships on a more southwesterly course. The admiral wished to discover if there were lands south of the Caribbean island of Dominica.

Soft Atlantic winds blew the ships toward the equator until, on July 13, they entered a region of calm weather and steaming heat. "The wind stopped so suddenly and unexpectedly," wrote Columbus, "and the . . . heat was so excessive . . . that there was no one who dared go below to look after the casks of wine and water, which burst, snapping the hoops."

Sea grape trees on the island of Dominica in the West Indies

In their woolen clothes the crews sweated and suffered for eight days until the wind picked up and fluffed the sails. Bounding once more over rolling waves, Columbus changed his course to due west. As always, some nervous sailors grumbled that the ships were traveling too far into unknown waters. But on July 31 the admiral correctly guessed they had reached the seas south of Dominica.

That very day Columbus happily recorded, "a seaman . . . named Alonso Perez, climbed to the crow's nest and saw land to the westward, distant 15 leagues, and it appeared to be in the shape of three rocks or mountains." During the outward voyage, Columbus had prayed regularly to the three figures of the Holy Trinity. Now, as if by a miracle, three mountains marked their first sight of land. In faithful gratitude, the admiral named the island Trinidad (The Trinity).

Map showing the many "mouths" of the Orinoco River

Sailing westward along Trinidad's southern coast, the sailors saw another island in the distance. Columbus called it Isla Sancta (Holy Island). It was one of the islands at the mouth of the great Orinoco River of present-day Venezuela. The admiral was gazing for the first time at the continent of South America.

Sailing onward, the fleet rounded the southwestern end of Trinidad on August 4. "Very late that night, when I was on deck," Columbus later exclaimed, "I heard a terrible roaring. . . . And I saw the sea rise . . . like a hill as high as the ship. . . ." Columbus expected the frightening wall of water to smash his ship at any moment. Instead it passed beneath, lifting the ship high into the air and then safely dropping it down. Perhaps the sudden current was floodwater gushing from the Orinoco River. Columbus named the place Boca de la Sierpe (The Serpent's Mouth).

Continuing northward, the fleet soon reached a strait that separated northwestern Trinidad from a long peninsula of the mainland. Rough currents flowed here, too, and Columbus named this strait Boca del Dragon (The Dragon's Mouth). Through the next days the fleet sailed along the peninsula's southern coast. The land rose into high mountains, and in the coastal jungles great swarms of monkeys swung about and chattered in the trees.

"I had not yet conversed with any people from these islands," wrote Columbus, "which I greatly desired to do." At last he anchored the fleet at the mouth of a river. "And immediately many people came, and they told me they called this land Paria." The Paria Peninsula is part of Venezuela today.

The natives of Paria possessed a culture more developed than that of the other Indians Columbus had met. They wore flattened circles of polished gold suspended from their necks. Native craftsmen also created nose rings and pendants from a mixture of copper and gold which they called *guanin*. Gladly the natives traded their jewelry for brass hawks' bells.

Sailing farther west, the seamen met other natives who wore pearl armbands and lustrous pearl necklaces. "I rejoiced greatly when I saw these things," admitted Columbus, "and spared no effort to find out where they obtained them, and they told me that they got them there and in a land farther north."

The fleet steered back to the Dragon's Mouth. After passing through that strait, the ships turned west and bounded along the northern coast of Paria. On August 15 they neared an island Columbus called Margarita. If the ships had landed there, the sailors might have discovered unbelievable treasures. The

North coast of Trinidad

Columbus at Margarita Island

oyster beds of Margarita would yield to future Spanish explorers great quantities of pearls. Columbus, however, ordered his ships to set a northerly course.

Weeks of constant sailing had weakened the forty-seven-year-old admiral. His joints ached with arthritis, and eyestrain seemed nearly to blind him. In his cabin he rubbed his bloodshot eyes and painfully scribbled his thoughts in his journal. Paria, he now claimed, lay at the edge of the Garden of Eden, earth's true paradise. "I have come to believe," he wrote, "that this is a vast continent hitherto unknown." For the first time Columbus suspected that instead of reaching Asia he had discovered "Otro Mundo," Another World.

Hardly able to stand upon deck, the sick admiral once again proved his amazing ability as a navigator. After sailing across uncharted Atlantic waters and crisscrossing along the unknown Paria coast, he confidently set a course to carry the fleet north to Hispaniola. Lookouts cheered when, sure enough, the peaks of Hispaniola rose on the horizon on August 19.

The fleet touched land about 150 miles (241 kilometers) west of the new capital, Santo Domingo. A few days later, a ship appeared sailing along the coast. It was commanded by Bartholomew Columbus. After a separation of two-and-a-half years, the two brothers warmly greeted each other. Bartholomew, however, brought the admiral unsettling news. Rebellion once again had broken out on Hispaniola.

View of the city of Santo Domingo

Obeying the admiral's parting instructions, Bartholomew had set the colonists to work building Santo Domingo. Illness, hunger, and suffering, however, had caused growing discontent among the settlers. Some seventy Spaniards led by Francisco Roldan suddenly announced their refusal to take any more orders from Bartholomew. Surging across the countryside in open revolt, Roldan's mob attacked an inland fort and looted the old settlement at Isabela. Then they settled into the island's unconquered southwestern region, called Xaragua, where they formed an alliance with a chieftain named Guarionex.

The three supply ships Columbus had sent directly to Hispaniola accidentally landed at Xaragua instead of Santo Domingo. Many crewmen quickly deserted and joined Roldan's rebels. A lazy life stretched out in a hammock seemed far more attractive than hard work in Santo Domingo. Protected by Roldan and Guarionex, many Indians refused to pay their taxes. Other lawless bands of Spaniards also roamed the island.

Wearily Christopher Columbus reached Santo Domingo on August 31, 1498. In October he sent two cargo-laden ships back to Spain. He penned a report of his latest discoveries and also described the disorder on Hispaniola. He asked that the king and queen send a royal judge out to the colony.

While awaiting action, Columbus spent the next long months making peace with Francisco Roldan. He promised to name Roldan mayor of Santo Domingo for life and offered all of the rebels pardon. Those who wished to sail home for Spain could do so as soon as possible. To the rest he granted land and houses in Xaragua. By a system called *repartimiento*, the island's natives were forced to work on these estates.

Peace with Roldan and his followers failed to bring calm to Hispaniola, however. Indian uprisings and bands of criminal Spaniards kept the admiral and his brothers fully occupied. At last, on August 23, 1500, a Spanish fleet appeared on the coast. On the deck of one ship stood the grave figure of Francisco de Bobadilla. Ferdinand and Isabella had named that stern nobleman governor of all the Indies, and they trusted in him to restore order and dispense "royal justice" on Hispaniola.

Full of his sense of duty, Bobadilla stepped ashore at Santo Domingo. Unhappily, the first sight that greeted his eyes was that of seven Spanish corpses dangling from gallows trees. Soon he learned that five more rebels were scheduled for hanging the next day.

Outraged at this apparent cruelty toward Spanish citizens, Bobadilla demanded that the prisoners be handed over to him. Christopher and Bartholomew Columbus were away at the moment battling Indians and rebel gangs. Diego Columbus, left in charge, refused to act without orders from the admiral. Furiously Bobadilla arrested Diego in the name of Ferdinand and Isabella.

The powerful new governor moved into the admiral's house and began issuing laws of his own. Those Spaniards in Santo Domingo who hated the foreign Columbus brothers quickly stepped forward with their stories and complaints. Soon Bobadilla had heard enough. Angrily he ordered Columbus to return to Santo Domingo. When the admiral respectfully obeyed this summons, Bobadilla welcomed him by clapping him in irons and locking him in the town jail. Bartholomew soon surrendered peaceably, only to be arrested as well.

Completely stunned, Columbus sat in his gloomy cell. Outside he heard the mocking laughter of his Santo Domingo enemies. "Things have come to such a pass," he wrote, "that there is none so vile as dare not insult me." He had served King Ferdinand and Queen Isabella to the best of his ability. As Admiral of the Ocean Sea, he had presented the Spanish monarchs with the western Indies, and this was his reward.

For several weeks Bobadilla collected testimony against the Columbus brothers and finally ordered that they be sent to Spain for trial. With silent dignity, Christopher Columbus stepped from jail. Still in chains, he boarded the caravel *La Gorda*, which set sail early in October 1500. Just eight years after landing at San Salvador, the great discoverer was being shipped home like a common criminal.

Columbus returning to Spain in chains aboard La Gorda

Chapter 10
The High Voyage

"**A**s soon as they had put to sea, the captain, who had learned of Bobadilla's hardness of heart, offered to free him of his chains, but this the admiral refused. He had been put in irons in the name of the Sovereigns, he said, and he would wear them until they gave orders for them to be removed." So wrote Ferdinand Columbus of this trying time in his father's life.

Ferdinand and his older brother Diego had often felt the sting of their father's spiteful enemies while they were royal pages at court. When they walked in the streets, unhappy sailors and colonists who had returned from the Indies often pointed and jeered, "There go the sons of the Admiral of the Mosquitoes!"

On November 20, 1500, *La Gorda* sailed into Cádiz harbor. Now Spaniards were prepared to taunt Columbus himself. But as the explorer slowly shuffled along the dock, weighted down with chains, people soon changed their minds. They reacted to the sorry sight with sympathy and outrage. This was no way to treat the Admiral of the Ocean Sea.

When Ferdinand and Isabella learned what had happened, they ordered the Columbus brothers released. On December 17 the admiral reported to the court at Granada. Humbly he fell to his knees and kissed the hands of the king and queen. "With tears, he implored them to forgive him for his errors," recorded the historian Gonzalo Oviedo. "And when they had listened to him, they comforted him with great gentleness." Queen Isabella supposedly burst into tears herself at the thought of the cruel treatment the admiral had received.

The Spanish rulers pardoned Columbus for his mistakes while governing Hispaniola, but they made no effort to restore his powers as governor and viceroy. Clearly they regretted having granted so much in their original contract with Columbus. During the next months, Columbus worked quietly at a desk in the monastery of Las Cuevas in Seville. He collected his personal documents and letters and put together what he called *The Book of Privileges*. It carefully described all the titles and income the king and queen had promised him. He also repeatedly petitioned Ferdinand and Isabella for ships so he might make a fourth voyage. In the great gulf beyond Cuba, the admiral hoped to find a passage leading at last to India.

Surely it galled Columbus to learn of the successes of other explorers. From Portugal, Vasco da Gama had journeyed successfully to India by sailing around the southern tip of Africa. Portuguese sailor Pedro Cabral had discovered Brazil. Some members of Columbus's earlier voyages, such as Vicente Yáñez Pinzón and Alonso de Hojeda, were excitedly exploring the vast coast of Venezuela. In time, the glowing reports of navigator Amerigo Vespucci, an Italian in

Explorer Vasco da Gama

the pay of Spain, would lead to the naming of both continents of America after him. While Columbus paced and fretted in Seville, these men were reaping riches and glory.

On February 13, 1502, a great Spanish fleet of thirty ships sailed for Hispaniola. The ships carried 2,500 men commanded by Nicolás de Ovando. Ferdinand and Isabella had named Ovando to take Bobadilla's place as governor of Hispaniola.

Columbus saw that he was deprived of that office, but the king and queen soon granted their Admiral of the Ocean Sea another chance to go exploring. In truth, they regarded Columbus with his *Book of Privileges* and his constant petitions as something of an embarrassment. Sent off to sea, he would no longer be a bother to them.

On May 9, 1502, Columbus excitedly sailed from Cádiz. His fleet was considerably smaller than Governor Ovando's: just four ships and 150 men. With him aboard his flagship, *La Capitana*, the admiral gladly took his thirteen-year-old son Ferdinand. His brother Bartholomew sailed on the *Santiago de Palos*, nicknamed the *Bermuda*. The other two ships that cut westward through the waves were *La Gallega* and the *Viscayno*. Columbus called this fourth voyage "The High Voyage." At the age of fifty, his hopes for fame and fortune remained as high as ever.

Columbus made the fastest Atlantic crossing of his career. From the Canary Islands the fleet reached Martinique, the next Caribbean island south of Dominica, in just twenty-one days. The admiral's royal instructions told him not to stop at Santo Domingo on his outward journey. His presence there could only stir up trouble among the colonists.

Amerigo Vespucci, whose name was given to the Americas

But Columbus disregarded this order and sailed to Santo Domingo anyway, arriving outside the harbor on June 29. He hoped to exchange the disappointing *Bermuda* for a more seaworthy vessel. In the sky and sea he also noticed signs that a hurricane was fast approaching. He wished a safe haven where his fleet could weather the storm.

Curtly Governor Ovando refused to allow Columbus's ships into the harbor. He also scoffed at the admiral's hurricane warning. Twenty-eight ships of the grand Spanish fleet were ready to return to Spain, and heedlessly Ovando ordered them to sail without further delay.

One of Columbus's crewmen, Diego Mendez, requesting help from the unfriendly Governor Ovando

Denied entry into the harbor, Columbus hurried his four ships along the coast in search of shelter. Perhaps he saw the white canvas sails of the larger fleet disappear to the east. As the homeward-bound ships rounded the eastern tip of Hispaniola on the evening of June 30, the sky suddenly turned black and a hard rain splattered. Shrieking hurricane winds rose up, ripping sails and splitting masts. The swirling storm whipped the sea into a killing froth. Before dawn, twenty-four ships had sunk or crashed upon the coast.

Among the five hundred people who drowned were the ex-governor Bobadilla, the former rebel leader Francisco Roldan, and the chieftain Guarionex. Some 2,000 pounds (907 kilograms) of Hispaniola gold also sank to the bottom of the sea. Three battered ships limped back to Santo Domingo to tell the shocking tale. Strangely, the only ship that sailed on to Spain was the one that had been assigned to carry 405 pounds (184 kilograms) of gold owed to Columbus as his share under royal contract. It is small wonder that the admiral's enemies whispered that he had raised the storm by evil magic.

At the mouth of a river west of Santo Domingo, Columbus's four ships had endured the hurricane. "The storm was terrible," he later declared. "During the night it badly damaged my ships, dragging them all away so that each feared that the others were lost." After crewmen repaired damaged rigging and pumped the four ships dry, the little fleet sailed westward, finally turning south on July 27. Just three days of bright skies and strong winds carried the ships across the gulf to the island of Bonacca near the coast of present-day Honduras in Central America.

Very soon the Spaniards chanced upon a large canoe paddled by dozens of natives and filled with native trade goods. Excitedly the admiral examined the many items produced in this newly discovered region. Young Ferdinand Columbus remembered seeing beautiful "blankets and sleeveless cotton tunics, embroidered and colored in various patterns . . . long wooden swords . . . [edged] with sharp flints which cut like steel . . . and axes . . . of good copper." These natives carried certain nutlike beans that they greatly prized. In future years, Europeans would also greatly value the hot beverage brewed from the cacao or cocoa bean.

Although these natives told Columbus of the civilized Mayan people to the northwest, he chose to sail in the opposite direction. Again the admiral mistakenly believed he had found China, and he hoped to find an open passage to India around to the east and south. Sailing eastward along the mainland coast proved a nearly impossible task. "I had the wind, and a terrible current, against me all the way," explained Columbus. Thirty-eight days of stormy weather also plagued the sailors. "Rain, thunder, and lightning never ceased," the admiral complained, "and it seemed as if the end of the world were at hand."

Finally, on September 14, the ships rounded a point of land and sailed southward into smoother waters. Columbus called the place Cabo Gracias a Dios (Cape of Thanks Be to God). The fleet passed along the coast of what today are the countries of Nicaragua and Costa Rica and reached a region called Veragua (present-day Panama). Here Columbus sailed back and forth in search of treasure and the passage to India.

During these weeks the admiral lay very ill with fever and swollen joints in a special cabin he had built upon the deck of *La Capitana*. His son Ferdinand remained a constant comfort to him, though. "As for work he did as much as if he had been a sailor for eighty years," Columbus proudly observed.

Not surprisingly, every moment of the voyage filled the teenager with wonder and excitement. Ferdinand Columbus joined the other crew members when they landed upon beaches and traded trinkets for the polished gold disks worn by the suspicious and fearful natives. At one spot the boy saw his first alligators. "In the harbor," he later exclaimed, "were vast great lizards. . . . They are so ravenous and cruel that if they find a man asleep ashore they will drag him into the water to devour him."

Columbus's "ravenous lizards" were alligators.

During November and December, tropical storms whipped across the water. "The wind would change," declared Ferdinand, ". . . with such terrible thunder and lightning that the men dared not open their eyes and it seemed the ships were sinking and the heavens coming down."

On December 13, a terrifying waterspout passed between two of the ships. "It would surely have swamped anything it struck," marveled Ferdinand, "for it raises the water up to the clouds in a column . . . twisting it about like a whirlwind."

On January 6, 1503, the fleet at last took refuge at the mouth of a river Columbus named the Belen (Bethlehem). The awful weather had left all four ships soggy and damaged.

The crews also unhappily discovered that the *teredos*, or shipworms, abundant in those waters were eating into the hulls. Weakened by these tunneling worms, the ships all badly leaked.

Encouraged by the plentiful gold his men collected from the local natives, Columbus decided to establish a settlement at Belen and develop mines. He would leave Bartholomew there in charge of eighty men while he sailed onward.

The Spaniards chopped down trees and built log cabins. A local chieftain named Quibian grew upset when he saw that the strangers meant to stay. In April, Quibian raised a warrior army and attacked the little settlement.

Frantically the surprised Spaniards fired their small cannons and crossbows. Captain Diego Tristan and three other sailors fell bloody victims to spears and arrows. The other colonists felt lucky to escape back to the fleet.

Sick and exhausted, Columbus abandoned his plan for a colony at Belen. The hopelessly worm-eaten hull of *La Gallega* forced the admiral to abandon that sinking ship, too. Worse troubles confronted the fleet as it pressed along the Veragua coast. The *Viscayno* proved so leaky it also had to be left behind. Now the anxious Spanish crews crowded aboard the two remaining ships.

Food supplies were low and Columbus knew the menace of the *teredo* dangerously threatened *La Capitana* and the *Bermuda*. Woefully he realized he had no choice but to sail directly for Santo Domingo, though he knew they would be unwelcome there.

The sailors lived on a diet of wormy biscuits. They wearily dropped asleep after long shifts at the pumps. Trade winds pushed the ships off course until, on May 13, they reached Cuba. For a week the crewmen hammered and patched, making hurried repairs. Then the battered ships put out to sea again.

Heavy rains and contrary winds made the journey toward Santo Domingo seem like a total nightmare. Worse yet, the boring *teredo* left the ships' hulls so full of holes they might break apart at any moment. Desperately Columbus now sailed south with the wind toward Jamaica. Reaching that island was their only hope for survival.

The sailors sighed with relief on June 23 when they reached the Jamaican coast. For two more days the ships limped along until Columbus selected a sheltered harbor he named Santa Gloria. The badly leaking *La Capitana* and *Bermuda* could travel no farther. Below their decks the seeping water steadily rose as the hulls settled into the sand. Columbus and his sailors were marooned.

Lava rock on the coast of Santo Domingo

Chapter 11
Death of the Discoverer

For weeks the stranded explorers exchanged beads and red caps with the local natives for a regular supply of fish, maize, and cassava bread. The hungry sailors also gladly munched upon Jamaican lizards and rats. Columbus realized the only hope for the rescue of his shipwrecked men would be to send for help. Bravely Diego Mendez and Bartolomeo Fieschi volunteered to lead an effort. With mixed crews of Spaniards and Indians, they paddled off in two canoes. These simple vessels would have to cross 500 miles (805 kilometers) of open sea in order to reach Hispaniola.

While they waited at Santa Gloria, the remaining sailors built huts of thatched palm leaves on the decks of the ships. Many men fell sick in these crowded conditions, and with his crippling arthritis Columbus could hardly hobble from his bed. Sadly he considered how low his "High Voyage" had sunk. "I am ruined," he mournfully declared, ". . . may Heaven pity me, and may the Earth weep for me."

Month after month passed with no sign of hope. Confined aboard ship, many of the castaways grew restless. Men grumbled that Mendez and Fieschi were surely lost. If they waited for Columbus to act, surely they would be lost, too. His anger and fear growing, Francisco de Porras, captain of the *Bermuda*, and his brother Diego gathered conspirators together. In whispered meetings these men agreed to mutiny.

At last on January 2, 1504, the moment for confrontation arrived. That morning Francisco de Porras barged into the admiral's cabin on *La Capitana*.

"Señor," threatened Porras, "do you wish to keep us here perishing?" Calmly Columbus offered to listen to any plan Porras might suggest. "It is no time for talk," rudely answered Porras. He shouted that he would go to Spain with anyone who would follow him.

That signal sparked the mutineers to action. "We're with you!" they yelled. "Kill the admiral and his men!" As dozens of rebels rushed over the deck, loyal sailors protected the admiral, Bartholomew Columbus, and young Ferdinand from harm.

Angrily the mutineers filled ten native canoes and paddled away. They hoped to journey across the sea to Hispaniola. When they failed to make progress, however, they landed again. Through the next months, the grizzled mob wildly roamed Jamaica living off the country.

With some fifty loyal sailors, many of them sick, Columbus remained with the ships wrecked at Santa Gloria. In time, the local natives tired of bringing food to the demanding Spaniards. Each day's supply grew smaller and smaller. Columbus saw that his men would starve unless something was done. In his cabin he leafed through his almanac. By a stroke of good fortune, he noticed that in three day's time, on February 29, 1504, there would be a total eclipse of the moon.

Solemniy Columbus summoned all of the local chieftains aboard *La Capitana*. He told them that God, whom the Christians worshipped, disapproved of the unfaithful Indians because they failed to bring food. As punishment, Columbus announced, God intended to blot out the moon.

Columbus and the dramatic eclipse of the moon

The moon rose as usual on the night of February 29. Just as Columbus predicted, it was soon swallowed by a dark red shadow. Along the beach, natives wailed with fear. They begged Columbus to have his God restore the moon. In time, the moon gradually returned to normal. Thereafter the terrified natives carried baskets brimming with fruits, fish, and cassava bread to the stranded ships every day.

Eight long months after Mendez and Fieschi paddled away toward Hispaniola, a small caravel appeared outside Santa Gloria. Amazingly, the two had succeeded in reaching Hispaniola. Now Governor Ovando was sending a caravel to see if the castaways were still alive. The captain of the ship, Diego de Escobar, refused to take aboard any of the shipwrecked men, however. He claimed his ship was too small. Instead he sailed away to report to Governor Ovando, who was glad, no doubt, that Columbus was marooned.

Still the shipwrecked men knew their friend Mendez would send real help as soon as possible. Full of good spirits, Columbus sent a messenger to the camp of the mutineers and offered them a general pardon. Instead of accepting forgiveness, the rowdy rebels chose to march against the admiral's loyal men. Bartholomew Columbus swiftly assembled the loyalists to meet this latest threat. Armed with swords and spears, the two sides clashed on May 19.

Furiously the loyal sailors slashed and jabbed, with their weapons striking down about six of the mutineers and capturing Francisco de Porras. "Seeing themselves so roughly handled," exclaimed Ferdinand Columbus, "those vile mutineers turned tail and ran away with all their might." Only one loyal sailor died in the bloody fight. Having put Francisco de Porras in chains, the admiral generously agreed to forgive the other rebels. Soon all of the mutineers surrendered and returned to the sunken ships to await rescue.

At last, on June 28, 1504, real help arrived at Santa Gloria. A caravel chartered by Diego Mendez picked up the surviving castaways. Some one hundred men with long beards and ragged clothes excitedly crowded aboard the ship. After one year and five days, Columbus and his stranded crews escaped from Jamaica. "As Columbus told me later in Spain," wrote Diego Mendez, "he had never in his life known so joyful a day, for he had never expected to leave that place alive."

Governor Ovando courteously greeted the admiral when the ship anchored at Santo Domingo in early August, but he set Francisco de Porras free. Columbus realized he would get no justice in Hispaniola. In September he boarded a ship bound for Spain along

Columbus welcoming the faithful Diego Mendez

with his brother, son, and other loyalists. Terrible storms broke the mainmast and the foremast during the long Atlantic voyage. Once more the Columbus brothers drew upon the best of their sailing skills to guide the damaged ship home. Finally on November 7, 1504, the explorers reached the coast of Spain at the port of Sanlucar de Barrameda.

Queen Isabella

The admiral had lost all four of his ships during his High Voyage. But he had made valuable discoveries and had brought home a large amount of gold. He had reason to hope, therefore, that the king and queen would be glad to learn of his return. Sadly, though, Queen Isabella lay on her deathbed. After a long illness, she died on November 26, 1504, at the age of fifty-three. "Her death caused the admiral much grief," remembered Ferdinand Columbus, "for she had always aided and favored him, while the King he always found somewhat reserved and unsympathetic to his projects."

Columbus's own health was failing rapidly. His arthritis left him lame and hardly able to move. The constant strain of a life at sea had broken his health forever. This was the price he paid for the glory of his discoveries. Perhaps he realized he would never return to sea. Now he wished only to protect the titles and privileges he had earned.

In a house in Seville attended by servants, the Admiral of the Ocean Sea lay bedridden. His shares of the gold diggings on Hispaniola enabled him to live comfortably. But he feared King Ferdinand did not intend to honor their contract fully. "I swear," he wrote to his son Diego at court, ". . . that the loss I am suffering . . . amounts to ten millions a year, and it can never be paid back."

King Ferdinand

In May 1505, Columbus dragged himself from bed. By mule he painfully rode to Segovia, where King Ferdinand was holding court. Vainly he petitioned the king to restore his full rights as governor and viceroy of all the Indies. The king agreed only to allow the archbishop of Castile to examine this request.

In October 1505 the royal court moved to Salamanca and in April 1506 to Valladolid. Both times Columbus followed along, hoping to press his petition. "Although this sickness is for the moment tormenting me unmercifully," he promised King Ferdinand, "I will still be able to serve You in such a manner as no man has yet seen."

His health grew steadily worse, however. In May 1506 the fifty-four-year-old explorer penned his last will. Clearly the end was near. Diego and Ferdinand stayed at their father's bedside. The admiral's friends Diego Mendez and Bartolomeo Fieschi also helped keep watch over him. Sorrowful about the loss of his rights and titles and in great pain from his arthritis, Christopher Columbus gave up his last stubborn struggle on May 20, 1506, at Valladolid. His dying words were words of faith: "O Lord, into Thy hands I commend my spirit."

The Admiral of the Ocean Sea was buried in Valladolid, although in 1509 the body was removed to Seville. Mourners watched as priests entombed the casket in the great cathedral there. That year the king appointed Columbus's son Diego governor of Hispaniola. In 1541 Columbus's bones were moved again. Shipped to Hispaniola, they were buried in the Santo Domingo cathedral. It seems right that Christopher Columbus should rest forever in the New World he discovered.

During his life Christopher Columbus suffered many failures and made numerous mistakes in judgment. He shall be remembered, however, for his daring and his strength. Bold ambition, keen insight, and incredible courage were the uncommon elements of his character. Driven by pride and dreams of wealth, the joy of discovery became his real reward, greater than all of the gold imaginable. The voyages of Columbus opened the pathways to the entire western hemisphere. Cortés, Pizarro, Balboa, Ponce de León, and all of the great explorers who followed, owe their fame to the man who first stepped upon the sandy shore of San Salvador in 1492, the master Genoese sailor Christopher Columbus.

The death of Columbus

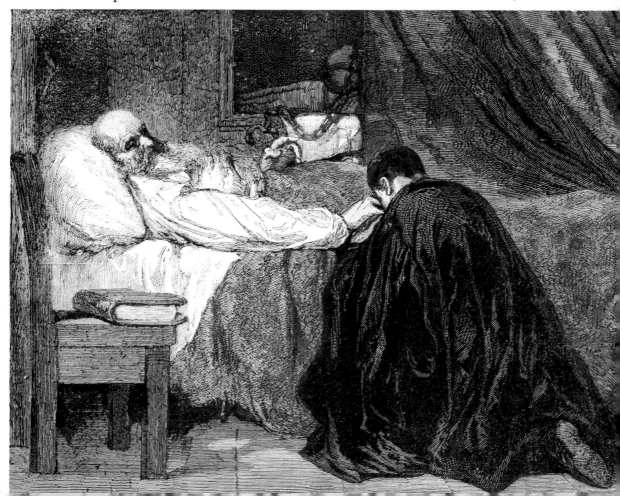

Appendix

Columbus's journals and letters give fascinating descriptions of the land and people of the Indies. At the same time, the reader can see some of the attitudes that led to colonization and slavery in the New World.

As soon as I arrived in the Indies, in the first island which I found, I took some of the natives by force, in order that they might learn and might give me information of whatever there is in these parts. At present, those I bring with me are still of the opinion that I come from Heaven . . .

They are the most handsome men and women whom [we] had found up to then, so very fair that, if they were clothed and protected themselves from the sun and air, they would be almost as white as the people of Spain, for this land is very cool and the best that tongue can describe.

In all these islands, it seems to me that all men are content with one woman. . . . It appears to me that the women work more than do the men.

They are . . . without any knowledge of war, and very cowardly, so that a thousand of them would not face three. And they are also fitted to be ruled and to be set to work, to cultivate the land and to do all else that may be necessary, and you [the king and queen] may build towns and teach them to go clothed and adopt our customs.

They are so guileless and so generous with all that they possess, that no one would believe it who has not seen it. They refuse nothing that they possess, if it be asked of them. . . . They are content with whatever trifle of whatever kind that may be given to them, whether it be of value or valueless. I forbade that they should be given things so worthless as fragments of broken crockery, scraps of broken glass and lace tips, although when they were able to get them, they fancied that they possessed the best jewel in the world.

They are the best people in the world and beyond all the mildest, so that I have much hope in Our Lord that Your Highnesses will make them all Christians, and that they will be all yours. . . .

Timeline of Events in Columbus's Lifetime

1451—Christopher Columbus (Colombo) is born in Genoa, Italy

1476—After jumping overboard in a sea battle, Columbus floats ashore in Lagos, Portugal, then moves to Lisbon

1477—Columbus sails into the North Atlantic; he joins his brother Bartholomew in the mapmaker's trade

1479—Columbus marries Felipa Moniz Perestrello; Ferdinand of Aragon and Isabella of Castile unite their kingdoms

1480—Columbus's son Diego is born

1484—Columbus proposes his westward voyage to the Indies to King John II of Portugal but is refused

1486—Columbus visits Ferdinand and Isabella of Spain to request support for his voyage

1488—Beatriz de Harana bears Columbus's second son, Ferdinand; Columbus again requests the support of King John II and is refused again; Bartolomeu Dias sails around the southern tip of Africa

1490—A Spanish royal commission advises that Columbus's scheme would not work

1492—Ferdinand and Isabella finally approve Columbus's voyage; he sets sail from Spain in August, spends a month on the Canary Islands, and lands on the Caribbean island of San Salvador on October 12; he leaves men behind to build the colony of La Navidad on Hispaniola

1493—With seventeen ships, Columbus sails from Cádiz on his second voyage to the New World; he founds the colony of Isabela on Hispaniola and explores the coasts of Cuba and Jamaica

1494—In the Treaty of Tordesillas, Spain and Portugal set the boundaries for their New World empires

1497—Englishman John Cabot reaches the North American mainland, probably at Labrador

1498—Columbus leaves for Hispaniola on his third voyage; he first sights and names Trinidad, then explores the Venezuelan coast; Vasco da Gama sails around Africa and reaches India

1499—Amerigo Vespucci sails across the Atlantic to the coast of Venezuela

1500—Governor Bobadilla of Hispaniola arrests Columbus and ships him back to Spain in chains; Pedro Cabral reaches the coast of Brazil and claims it for Portugal

1501—Vasco Núñez de Balboa sails to Hispaniola

1502—Columbus sails from Cádiz on his fourth voyage; he explores the coast of Central America

1503—Their ships worm-eaten, Columbus and his crew are marooned on Jamaica

1504—Columbus is rescued and sails back to Spain

1506—Christopher Columbus dies in Valladolid, Spain, on May 20

Glossary of Terms

algae—Filmy or leafy aquatic plants, many of which are red or brown instead of green

almanac—A book with tables and charts giving forecasts on astronomy and climate for each day or week of the year

arthritis—A painful swelling of the joints

boatswain—A ship's officer in charge of maintenance and repair of the ship's hull

cannibal—A person or animal that eats the flesh of its own species

caravel—A small, wide sailing ship, usually with three masts

chandler—A merchant who provides equipment and supplies for a specific kind of venture

chaperone—A person who accompanies an unmarried couple to make sure they behave properly

constellation—A pattern that seems to be formed by a group of stars

crow's nest—A lookout platform on the top of a ship's mast

dead reckoning—A method of navigating by analyzing the direction and speed of the ship and the water's currents

doublet—A jacket worn by European men in the 15th–16th centuries

dowry—Money or property that a woman gives to her husband in marriage

flagship—The ship that carries the fleet's captain and flies his flag

grappling hook—An iron hook used to anchor boats, grasp underwater objects, or snare another ship

hawks' bells—Bells that falconers attached to hunting birds

helmsman—The person at the helm; the one who steers the ship

hold—The part of a ship below deck where cargo is kept

lateen sail—A triangular sail extended at the bottom by a long spar

leadsman—A sailor who lowers a piece of lead to determine the water's depth

marooned—Isolated in a desolate place with no hope of escape

Middle Ages—European historic period from about A.D. 500 to 1500

mutiny—A revolt of a ship's crew against the captain's authority

packet boat—A boat that carries cargo and mail

page—A boy serving at court or training to be a knight

poop deck—A small deck above a ship's main rear deck

reef—A ridge of rock or coral just under the water's surface

reef sails—To roll up sails so that they present a smaller surface area to the wind

stern—The rear end of a boat

superstitious—Believing in falsehoods through ignorance or fear

tiller—The handle attached to a ship's rudder

trade winds—Winds in a certain location that blow in one direction all the time

viceroy—A governing official who is the representative of a king

waterspout—A tunnel-shaped cloud that whips up water on the surface of the ocean

yardarm—The end of the pole running across the bottom of a sail

Bibliography

For further reading, see:

Collis, John S. *Christopher Columbus*. Briarcliff Manor, NY: Stein & Day, 1977.

Colon, Fernando. *The Life of the Admiral Christopher Columbus by His Son Ferdinand*. Translated by Benjamin Keen. New Brunswick, NJ: Rutgers University Press, 1959.

De Vorsey, Louis, Jr., and Parker, John, editors. *In the Wake of Columbus: Islands and Controversy*. Detroit, MI: Wayne State University Press, 1985.

Granzotto, Gianni. *Christopher Columbus*. Garden City, NY: Doubleday, 1985.

The Journal of Christopher Columbus. Translated by Cecil Jane. NY: Bonanza Books, 1960.

McKendrick, Melveena, and the editors of Horizon Magazine. *Ferdinand and Isabela*. NY: American Heritage Publishing Co., 1968.

Morison, Samuel Eliot. *Admiral of the Ocean Sea: A Life of Christopher Columbus*. Boston, MA: Little, Brown, 1942.

Index

Page numbers in boldface type indicate illustrations.

Picture Identifications for Chapter Opening Spreads

6-7—Columbus coasting along the northern shore of Cuba
14-15—Genoa, Italy, birthplace of Christopher Columbus
22-23—The Alhambra, the Moorish fortress in Granada, Spain
34-35—Columbus's ships on his first voyage to the Americas, by Rafael Monleon; in the Naval Museum, Madrid, Spain
48-49—Columbus's first landing in the New World
60-61—Juan de la Cosa's map, the first to show the Caribbean
68-69—Sunset through the palms, Dominican Republic
80-81—Brown pelicans at sunset
92-93—Blue-gray tanager, Trinidad
104-105—Croton shrub of the Bahamas
114-115—Runaway Bay, Jamaica

Acknowledgment

For a critical reading of the manuscript, our thanks to John Parker, Ph.D., Curator, James Ford Bell Library, University of Minnesota, Minneapolis, Minnesota.

Picture Acknowledgments

The Bettmann Archive—31, 44, 46
Steven Gaston Dobson—Cover illustration
Historical Pictures Service, Chicago—2, 19, 25, 27, 40, 47, 53 (margin), 57, 71, 72, 73 (bottom), 106, 107, 119
Journalism Services—11, 28, 30 (margin)
North Wind Picture Archives—6-7, 9, 10, 12, 13, 14-15, 16, 21, 29, 30 (top), 42, 43, 45, 51, 55, 59, 62 (bottom), 63, 65, 67, 73 (top), 74, 75, 79, 82, 83, 86, 87, 89, 91, 94, 97, 99, 100, 103, 109, 117, 118, 120, 121
Odyssey Productions: 17, 20, 70; © Robert Frerck—2, 5, 31 (margin), 33, 34-35, 37, 38, 41, 48-49, 50, 60-61
Root Resources: © Earl L. Kubis—52 (bottom)
Tom Stack & Associates: © M. Timothy O'Keefe—84 (top)
© **Lynn M. Stone**—76, 111
Tony Stone Worldwide/Chicago Ltd.: © Robert Frerck—22-23, 39; © Carol Lee—113
Valan Photos: © John Cancalosi—80-81; © Kennon Cooke—84 (bottom), 114-115; © Ian Davis-Young—68-69; © Jeff Foote—62 (top); © Harold V. Green—96; © Pam E. Hickman—92-93, 98; © Paul L. Janosi—52 (top); © Pierre Kohler—104-105; © R. La Salle—53 (top); © Robert C. Simpson—85

About the Author

Zachary Kent grew up in Little Falls, New Jersey, graduated from St. Lawrence University, and holds a teaching certificate in English. He worked for a New York City literary agency for two years before launching his writing career. To support himself while writing, he has worked as a taxi driver, a shipping clerk, and a house painter. Mr. Kent has had a lifelong interest in history. His special hobby as a boy was the study of United States presidents. His collection of presidential items includes books, pictures, and games, as well as several autographed letters.